THE BIBLE'S WAYS OF PRAYER

THE BIBLE'S WAYS

OF PRAYER

Wilfrid Harrington, O.P.

Michael Glazier, Inc.
Wilmington, Delaware 19801

First published in 1980 by

MICHAEL GLAZIER, INC.
1210 King Street
Wilmington, Delaware 19801

Library of Congress Catalog Number: 80-82827

International Standard Book Number: 0-89453-182-4

Printed in the United States of America

CONTENTS

In Memory of
Two Brothers

JEREMIAH — my Father
JOHN   my Uncle

Preface

A heartening feature of our day is an interest in prayer. People are praying again. And their prayer is not out of prayerbooks. They pray in their own words. The purpose of this book is to encourage a happy trend.

We might expect that the Bible will have something to teach us about prayer. The Bible is, after all, a meetingplace of God and man, of the Father and his children. There we learn of God's demand and man's response. Prayer is an intimate answer to the call of God.

What may surprise us Christians is the naturalness of the prayer of Israel. Old Testament men and women spoke straightforwardly to their God. And they turned to him with a refreshing boldness. Theirs is no God of terror but a God who is very personal and very near. We have much to learn from that prayerful people.

As a son of Israel, Jesus prayed. As Son of God he taught us to pray. As risen Lord he became the focus of prayer. Example, teaching, inspiration: he is ground and goal of our prayer.

Our first brothers and sisters in the faith—sons and daughters of Israel—were already people of prayer. Their Christian experience gave a fresh intimacy to their intercourse with God, now their Abba. They turned to the Son with easy grace. And the Spirit gave substance to their prayer.

The Bible is a school of prayer. If we would learn we must be open and docile. And learn we can if we have the will. After all, those who worked with God in bringing about this word of God knew something of God. We can safely trust their guidance and walk in their way to find and come to the Father.

Wilfrid Harrington, O.P.

I. The Old Testament

Introduction

Before one can answer the question, What is prayer? one must have come to terms with the question of God. One cannot pray to an Unmoved Mover. Prayer to a Pure Spirit will not have much body to it. Prayer is a meeting of persons—of the human person and the Person who is God. Old Testament man, we shall see, had a keen awareness of the personhood of God, a God who was the Father of Abraham and Isaac and Jacob. That is why he could pray so readily and so well.

We Christians know that we ought to pray. Our Lord himself had made that quite clear in his practice and in his teaching. We may not quite appreciate that his emphasis on prayer is not something new; it is not at all surprising in one who was a son of Israel. The truth is that the Israelites can teach us more than a little about prayer. We Christians know that we ought to pray, but we are not notably good at praying.

From the start of my scriptural studies my inclination has been towards the New Testament. But, during a teaching career of some twenty years and more, I have had, regularly, to give courses in the Old Testament. For some time now I have been conscious that this has been a blessing. I have developed an attachment to the Old Testament and an unbounded admiration for the men and women of Israel. I have become more convinced that a practical neglect of the Old Testament has not been helpful to Christians. Nor, for that matter, has the tendency to turn it into a Christian book by ignoring its distinctive character. I am sure that we undervalue the Old Testament to our own loss. If, for instance, one wishes to learn about prayer and turns at once or exclusively to the New Testament, one will miss out on a whole exhilarating dimension.

It has long been recognized that to take a theme and follow it through either Testament must lead to a better understanding of the Bible. It could not be otherwise with a theme as basic and central as prayer. My procedure in this Old Testament part of the book is quite straightforward: I take, one by one, the sections of the Old Testament structure. One learns that though emphases differ according to circumstances, the earnestness and quality of prayer are sustained. From listening to Israelites at prayer one cannot fail to learn how to pray.

Prayer will differ according to the status and role of those who pray. Patriarchs, leaders—and prophets too —are intercessors and they know the responsibility and the cost of intercession. A prophet is one who has had an experience, one might call it a mystical experience, of God. A Jeremiah shows what that can do for one's prayer. The men of wisdom of Israel were just that: wise men. The source of their wisdom was their commitment to God. They were, necessarily, men of prayer. It is common experience that affliction may drive one to prayer. Some, at least, of those who had experienced the downfall of Judah, and their children who lived as a subject people, came to see their God and themselves in a stark new light and gave vent to that knowledge in their prayers. The women of Israel were never less faithful or fervent than their menfolk; their prayers are as personal and as intense. The liturgical prayer-book of Israel—the Psalter—contains, among the 150 psalms, some that are personal prayers. From first to last, the Old Testament, with its many lessons, is a worthy school of prayer.

One

Prayer of the Fathers

"I am the God of Abraham, the God of Isaac, and the God of Jacob" (Ex 3:6). Looking at its distant past, a later Israel had drawn a stylized picture of its origins. Abraham was *the* father-figure who had received the divine promise of posterity and a homeland. The promise was renewed to his son Isaac and his grandson Jacob (also named Israel). The twelve sons of Jacob-Israel were the fathers of the twelve tribes of the people of Israel. The God of Abraham was the God of his descendants—and none other than the God who had revealed to Moses his name Yahweh (Ex 6:2-3). This neat construct expresses a people's awareness of its ethnic identity, and is a profession of its faith (Genesis).

God's promise to Abraham seemed to have reached an impasse in Egyptian slavery. Then Moses was raised up: recipient of revelation, deliverer, the forger of a nation. Through him, Yahweh, "with a mighty hand and an outstretched arm" set his people free. God will always have the last word (Exodus–Deuteronomy).

In the heading of this chapter I have avoided the term "patriarchs" simply because Moses is not usually so designated—the traditional patriarchs being Abraham, Isaac and Jacob. But Moses is, more truly than they, the father of his people. And, in the matter of prayer, he has the most to teach us.

The Yahwist, who undoubtedly knew of the tradition that linked the revelation of the name Yahweh firmly to Moses, has his own way of asserting that the Creator God and the God of his own Yahwistic religion were one and the same: he simply uses the name "Yahweh" from the start. Moreover he claims that at the time of Enosh ("man"), son of Seth, "men began to call upon the name of Yahweh" (Gen. 4:26). This is the Bible's first reference to prayer.

Abraham

In Genesis 20 we find one of three versions of a familiar story in which a patriarch, at a foreign court, in order to protect himself, passed off his wife (whose beauty is extolled) as his sister (see 12:10–20; 26:1–11). In our passage Abraham emerges as an intercessor pleading for the prince Abimelech (20: 17). We shall learn that the intercessory role of Abraham (and of Moses) highlights an important aspect of biblical prayer. It was taken for granted that God had endowed some of his servants with a special grace of efficacious intercession. This is a gift which may cost its possessor dear, as we shall see in the case of Moses.

Abraham, in prayer, displays a refreshing outspokenness. Look at his plea for the people of Sodom. We catch the flavor of a bargaining bout in an oriental bazaar with prices being ruthlessly slashed. Abraham's clever opening gambit is designed to put Yahweh on the defensive. There is a smack of blackmail: Yahweh is surely not going to wipe out the righteous!

> Wilt thou indeed destroy the righteous with the wicked? Suppose there are fifty righteous within the city; wilt thou then destroy the place and not spare it for the fifty righteous who are in it? Far be it from thee to do such a thing, to slay the righteous with the wicked, so that the

righteous fare as the wicked! Far be that from thee! Shall
not the Judge of all the earth do right? (18: 23–25)

This is putting it up to Yahweh and no mistake. And, having made his point, Abraham is prepared to lower his
price: forty-five, forty, thirty, twenty, ten. He realizes that
lower than ten he cannot go and so the matter rests. But he
had made a valiant try (18: 22–33).

Jacob

The Jacob-stories of Genesis show him to be very different from Abraham. He is quite the con-man: deceiving
his father Isaac (27: 5–29) and placating his estranged
brother Esau at the end (32: 1–21). And he readily outwits
his equally unscrupulous uncle, Laban (see 29: 15–25;
30: 25–43). Yet, Jacob has his better moments. One of
them is the intriguing episode of "Jacob's ladder"
(28: 10–28). Bethel, where the scene is set, is a shrine that
marks a privileged meetingplace of God and man. There
God's messengers hurry up and down, from earth to
heaven, bearing petitions and responses. Small wonder
that Jacob exclaimed:

> How awesome is this place! This is none other than the
> house of God, and this is the gate of heaven (28: 17).

If we follow the Genesis sequence, the Bethel episode
worked a real change in Jacob. It may be, of course, that
the prospect of meeting with his brother Esau really scares
him. At any rate, in his urgent prayer to God, he strikes a
rare note of humility:

> I am not worthy of the least of all the steadfast love and all
> the faithfulness which thou hast shown to thy servant, for
> with only my staff I crossed the Jordan; and now I have
> become two companies. Deliver me, I pray thee, from the
> hand of my brother, from the hand of Esau, for I fear him
> (32: 10–11).

If the Bethel episode rings strangely, another Jacob incident is plainly bizarre. Jacob had sent his family and flocks
across the imposing Jabbok River in Transjordan.

> And Jacob was left alone; and a man wrestled with him un-
> til the breaking of the day. When the man saw that he did
> not prevail against Jacob, he touched the hollow of his
> thigh, and Jacob's thigh was put out of joint as he wrestled
> with him. Then he said, "Let me go, for the day is break-
> ing." But Jacob said, "I will not let you go, unless you
> bless me." And he said to him, "What is your name?" And
> he said, "Jacob." Then he said, "Your name shall no more
> be called Jacob but Israel, for you have striven with God
> and with men, and have prevailed!" Then Jacob asked
> him, "Tell me, I pray you, your name." But he said, "Why
> is it that you ask my name?" And there he blessed him. So
> Jacob called the name of the place Peniel, saying, "For I
> have seen God face to face, and yet my life is preserved"
> (32: 24–30).

This is a Yahwistic passage and, typically, reflects older
tradition. In an earlier version of the story the
"man,"quite likely, had been a river-god. As the Yahwist
presents the episode he is none other than Yahweh. Bruce
Vawter has caught the significance of the passage: "At the
risk of oversimplification, we would suggest that the biblical message of the story lies in v. 29. 'Then Jacob asked
him, "Tell me, I pray, your name?" But he said, "Why is it
that you ask my name?" And there he blessed him.' A
Jacob previously adept at dealing with men (Esau, Isaac,
Laban, and soon Esau again) has now *contended with* God
and has similarly *prevailed* in a way that this tale can hard-
ly adequately explain but can only symbolize. Jacob had
an experience of the divine that has changed him (his limp,
v. 31, is an at least temporary reminder of the change). In
the chapters that follow he will assume both as an individual and as the embodiment of the Israel to come a
worthier posture of a man more sensitive to the higher
values both human and divine.... At the same time, he
has learned that a genuine relationship with God does not

reside in mere passivity, rejoicing in election and waiting
on providence (the prayer in vv 10-13); it entails as well
personal effort, a striving, wrestling with the divine will
and purposes." (B. Vawter, *On Genesis: A New Reading*;
New York: Doubleday, 1977, p. 351.)

At the close of Genesis, a Jacob, who had once selfishly
stolen a blessing, shows himself generous in the lavish
blessing of his grandchildren (48: 15-16, 20) and his sons
(49: 1-27).

Moses

We have noted the forthrightness of an Abraham. We
shall see, later, in Jeremiah and Job, striking instances of
outspokenness in addressing God—an approach
outrageous in its boldness. It ought not surprise us to
discover the same trait in the great servant of God, Moses.
He, like the others, makes no bones about complaining to
God. But he is never self-centered. He is very conscious of
his role of intercessor, his service to his people. Yet, as candidly as Job or Jeremiah, Moses complains:

> O Lord, why have you done evil to this people? Why did
> you ever send me? For since I came to Pharaoh to speak in
> your name, he has done evil to this people, and you have
> not delivered your people at all (Ex 5: 22-23).

You have not delivered your people at all! Moses had been
given a task, and he feels let down because there has been
no help from heaven. He is all the more annoyed because
God had hearkened to him when he interceded for
Pharaoh (8: 12-13, 29-31; 9: 33; 10: 16-19). He was learn-
ing the hard way what all who serve the God of Moses have
to learn in their turn: that the ways of God are not the
ways of man.

Moses was an intercessor—see Ex 15: 25; 17: 11-16. But
he is, too, a supreme example of the truth that God's gift
of efficacious intercession is one which may cost its

possessor dear. We discover, in the Exodus episode of the golden calf, an instance of the heroic generosity of Moses the intercessor:

> Moses said to the people, "You have sinned a great sin. And now I will go up to the Lord, perhaps I can make atonement for your sin." So Moses returned to the Lord and said, "Alas, this people have sinned a great sin; they have made for themselves gods of gold. But now, if thou wilt forgive their sins—and if not, blot me, I pray thee, out of thy book which thou has written" (Ex 32: 30-32).

Moses, conscious of his responsibility, is prepared to put his neck on the block. It is highly reminiscent of Paul who, many centuries later, in his turn still pleads for the "hard-necked" people:

> For I could wish that I myself were accused and cut off from Christ for the sake of my brethren, my kinsmen by race (Rom. 9: 3).

No trace here of "I'll keep you in my prayers!" The intercessor enters into the anguish of the situation and lays himself open to God.

Soon, in Exodus, we encounter again refreshing candor and a truly heartening ring of blackmail. Heartening because it is honest, and "honest blackmail" smacks of the paradox that must mark any encounter between God and mankind. Here Moses reminds God that words, even the words of God, are not enough; there must be some action!

> Thou hast said, "I know you by name, and you have also found favor in my sight." Now, therefore, I pray thee, if I have found favor in thy sight, show me now thy ways, that I may know thee and find favor in thy sight. Consider too that this nation is thy people (33: 12-13).

This is one of those Old Testament passages which make us Christians almost despair. We are disciples of the One who has become one of us (Jn 1: 14), of the high priest, like us in all things, who intercedes for us (Heb. 2: 17; 7: 25), of the one who has shown to us our prodigal Father (Lk 15: 11-32). Yet, this candor of Moses puts us to shame. He challenges his God with a boldness that we find distasteful, or worse: You have declared that I have found favor with you; very well, it is high time that you let me see a bit of that favor! And, in any case, this perverse crowd that I am trying to bring to their senses, is *your* people. *You* might try looking after them for a change! Surely, God has a sense of humor and would have appreciated the earthiness of this Moses. And, surely, ignorance of, or misunderstanding of, the Old Testament has, as much as anything, contributed to the drabness, and to the harshness, of much of historical Christianity

In the book of Numbers we find again how well Moses can complain to his God—just as vehemently as a later great servant of the Lord, Jeremiah.

> Why have you dealt ill with your servant? And why have I not found favor in your sight, that you lay the burden of all this people upon me? Did I conceive all this people? Did I bring them forth, that you should say to me, "Carry them in your bosom, as a nurse carries the sucking child, to the land which you did swear to give their fathers"? Where am I to get meat to give all this people? For they weep before me and say, "Give us meat, that we may eat." If you will deal thus with me, kill me at once, if I have found favor in your sight, that I may not see my wretchedness (Num 11: 11-15).

Moses is thoroughly fed-up with playing nursemaid to *God's* people. Death seems preferable to that thankless task. He speaks his mind without inhibition.

God, of course, holds the trump card. He threatens to destroy the rebellious people and make Moses the father of his new people. But Moses, for all his previous complaining, will not have it that way and pleads manfully for the people (how God must have smiled!):

The Egyptians will hear of it, and they will tell all the inhabitants of this land. . . . The nations will say, "Because the Lord was not able to bring this people into the land which he swore to give to them, therefore he has slain them in the wilderness. . . ." Pardon the iniquity of this people, I pray thee, according to the greatness of thy steadfast love, and according as you have forgiven this people from Egypt even until now (Num 14: 13-14, 16, 19).

This is sheer blackmail, of course. God will make himself a laughingstock if he permits his people to perish. Not much of a god he is, the nations will say, if he is unable to protect his own. We have something of the same in Ezekiel (cf. Ezek 36: 21-23). Again we should find this robust manner refreshing and not indulge in the questionable luxury of scandal. What ultimately matters is that Moses (like Jeremiah), for all his carping, is faithful to his calling. He will be nursemaid—if that is what God wants.

DEUTERONOMY

Deuteronomy teaches us that there is nothing magical about prayer, that it is always in keeping with God's purpose for us, a purpose that is supremely free. One would have expected that Moses, who had so faithfully guided God's people, and had suffered so fully in the process, would have led them, at last, into the Promised Land. And Moses, in thoroughly human fashion, yearned for just that privilege. He pleads:

O Lord God, thou hast only begun to show thy servant thy greatness and thy mighty hand; for what god is there in heaven or on earth who can do such works and mighty acts as thine? Let me go over, I pray, and see the good land beyond the Jordan, that goodly hill country, and Lebanon (Dt 3: 24-25).

But it was not to be. Moses, the faithful servant, was not to set foot in the land (3: 26-29). We cry "foul" and become indignant. That is because we *will* insist in holding a human scale against God's ways. We should accept that his ways will always overlap our measure. Why did God treat Moses so shabbily—as we imagine it? It is enough to quote the verdict of Deuteronomy on Moses:

> And there has not arisen a prophet since in Israel like Moses, whom the Lord knew face to face (34:10).

One is reminded of an assessment of the Baptist: "Truly, I say to you, among those born of woman, there has arisen no one greater than John the Baptist; yet he who is least in the kingdom of heaven is greater than he" (Mt 11: 11). After that solemn attestation, there is no questioning the peerless stature of John. Yet he, also, was not privileged to enter the promised land. In their fashion—and John more closely—Moses and John had already walked the way of God's most faithful Servant, a way that led to the cruel loneliness of, and to the foolishness of, the cross (Mk 15:34; 1 Cor 1:23). Moses, like John, has his privileged place apart. But he learned that fulfillment was not here. The scandal of the cross reaches back into the Old Testament.

We have noted above the role of an intercessor and have looked to its cost. Here, in Deuteronomy, that cost is brought out, quite forcefully. In face of the episode of the golden calf (see Ex 32), that grievous sin of the people, Moses forces the hand of the Lord by bringing all his intercessory power to bear.

> Then I lay prostrate before the Lord, forty days and forty nights. I neither ate bread nor drank water, because of all the sin which you had committed, in doing what was evil in the sight of the Lord, to provoke his anger. . .But the Lord hearkened to me that time also (9: 18-19).

Moses really had to work at being an intercessor, he had to pay the price. But his prayer has about it both a ring of confidence and a delicious smack of blackmail. The God to whom such a prayer is addressed is no ogre. He is a God

in whom we can discern the lineaments of the Prodigal
Father (cf. Lk 15: 11-32).

> I prayed to the Lord, "O Lord God, destroy not thy people
> and thy heritage, whom thou hast redeemed through thy
> greatness, whom thou hast brought out of Egypt with a
> mighty hand. Remember thy servants, Abraham, Isaac and
> Jacob; do not regard the stubbornness of this people, or
> their wickedness, or their sin, lest the land from which
> thou didst bring us say, 'Because the Lord was not able to
> bring them into the land which he promised them, and
> because he hated them, he has brought them out to slay
> them in the wilderness.' For they are thy people and thy
> heritage, whom thou didst bring out by thy great power
> and by thy outstretched arm." (Dt 9: 26-29)

After that, the Lord really had not much option! We need
to have in mind, of course, that Moses is not in the least
self-seeking. We might imagine him thinking of his job,
anxious to hang on. But we have seen that Moses had been
offered the chance of fathering a new people of God and
had turned it down flat (Num 14: 11-12). He is being wholly disinterested in this plea for the people. And his
unselfish prayer cannot fail to capture God's hearing and
win God's response.

Deuteronomy closes with the great hymn (Dt 32) which
is, if only in fragment, part of our Christian prayer (The
Divine Office), and with Moses' blessing on the tribes of
Israel. These blessings have their beauty and their comfort.
Israel is assured:

> The eternal God is your dwelling place, and underneath are
> the everlasting arms (33:27).

And one can savor the benediction:

> Happy are you, O Israel! Who is like you,
> a people saved by the Lord,
> the shield of your help,
> and the sword of your triumph! (33:29)

We may fittingly conclude this chapter, which has focused on the prayer of Moses, with the beautiful blessing which the priests were to learn from Moses:

> The Lord bless you and keep you:
> The Lord make his face to shine upon you, and be gracious to you:
> The Lord lift his countenance upon you, and give you peace (Numbers 6: 24-26).

Two

Prayer of the Leaders

Moses had brought the people to the border of the Promised Land; it was Joshua who led them into that land "flowing with milk and honey." They were in the land; possession of the land was another matter. At first local charismatic leaders—the "Judges"— did battle on a limited scale when groups of the settlers were threatened. It needed a man of David's caliber to win full control of the whole land. (Joshua, Judges).

David established a dynasty. More importantly, he, like Abraham before him, was recipient of a divine promise (1 Samuel 7): his kingdom was established and would abide. Solomon, his son, building on the achievement of his father, established Jerusalem more firmly as the religious focus of the nation by his imposing Temple. Sadly, the monarchy did not live up to its promise and the house of David was brought to an end by Nebuchadnezzar in 587 B.C. (1, 2 Samuel; 1, 2 Kings).

It was not the end of David. A later writer, the third-century Chronicler, saw that the divine promise had not been thwarted. That promise remained and would be fulfilled in God's good time, if in unsuspected ways (1, 2 Chronicles). But a new crisis, this time sparked by the Seleucid king, Antiochus IV, threatened again the nation and the promise. The hero, Judas Maccabeus, was the instrument of God's salvation (1, 2 Maccabees).

We speak here of *homo faber*, man the artisan. Biblical man was, spontaneously, *homo orans*—man who prayed to his God. Prayer is not a prerogative of the Fathers; it is, in Israel, a simple fact of life. It is salutary for us Christians to acknowledge that the Old Testament has much to teach us—not least in the area of prayer.

JOSHUA

The close of Deuteronomy asserts that "Joshua the son of Nun was full of the spirit of wisdom, for Moses had laid his hands upon him" (Dt 34: 9). He was assured that he would not be left without support as he stepped into Moses' shoes—the Lord would be with him (Jos 1: 1-9). He learned, quickly enough, that he, too, must be an intercessor, and must pay a price. After an attack on Ai had gone disastrously wrong, "Joshua rent his clothes, and fell to the earth upon his face before the ark of the Lord until the evening" (7: 6). His prayer, however, could not only win mercy for his people. It could bring sun and moon to a standstill in the heavens (10: 12-14).

JUDGES

Those charismatic leaders (the Judges) who, after the age of Joshua, from time to time led a tribe or group of tribes, also turned to Yahweh for help. Gideon, frightened by the task laid upon him (Jdg 6: 11-18), wants to be very sure indeed that the Lord is with him. When offered a sign he must make assurance double sure (6: 36-40). Later, the people take the stage and confess their sin—in dialogue with the Lord (10: 10-16). Their prayer: "We have sinned; do with us whatever seems good to thee; only deliver us, we pray thee, this day" (10: 15) anticipates the elaborate confessional prayers of post-exilic Judaism.

There is the strange story of the birth of Samson. A "man of God"—a heavenly visitor—had appeared to the wife of a Danite named Manoah and announced that,

though she had been hitherto childless, she would soon
have a son. When she told her husband, he gave voice to a
moving prayer:

> O Lord, I pray thee, let the man of God whom thou didst
> send come again to us, and teach us what we are to do with
> the boy that will be born (13: 8).

That boy grew up to be a parish hero who carried on a one-
man war against the Philistines. He was no saint, and has
been, not unfairly, described as "a great wenching lout"
who met his nemesis in Delilah (Chs 14-16). The prayer of
Samson in his bitter strait is quite in keeping with the kind
of person he is pictured as having been:

> O Lord God, remember me, I pray thee, only this once, O
> God, that I may be avenged upon the Philistines for one of
> my two eyes (16:28).

1-2 SAMUEL

With Samuel we move to a different level. Like Moses,
he is the intercessor (1 Sam 6: 5), a role not only
acknowledged by the people, but demanded by them: "Do
not cease to cry to the Lord our God for us, that he may
save us from the hand of the Philistines" (7: 8; 12: 19).
Samuel assures the people that he will not fail them: "Far
be it from me that I should sin against the Lord by ceasing
to pray for you" (12: 23). His stance is all the more
generous when we recall that he himself was opposed to the
institution of the monarchy. Yet he now intercedes for a
people who demand a king that they may be like all the nations (cf 8: 5).

David was something of a womanizer. It is perhaps fitting that his first recorded prayer should be one of
thanksgiving for his meeting with a woman who would
soon become his wife. He had been angered by the boorish
conduct of the surly Nabal and was preparing to teach him

a drastic lesson (1 Sam 25: 1-13). The man's wife, Abigail, took matters into her own hands. Her astuteness and, we presume, her charms, prevailed on David (25: 18-30).

> And David said to Abigail, "Blessed be the Lord, the God of Israel, who sent you this day to meet me!" (25: 32).

David's days of flight and forced brigandage came to an end. He became king, first of Judah, and then of the united kingdom of Judah and Israel. He had won for himself the city of Jerusalem and had made it his capital (2 Sam 5). By installing the ark of Yahweh there he turned it into the religious center of his domain (Ch. 6). Then, adverting to the incongruity that he had a palace while the ark of Yahweh was still housed in a tent, he planned to build a temple, but was told by the prophet Nathan that the temple was not to be his achievement. The Lord had pre-empted his plan. David had hoped to build a *house* (temple) for Yahweh; instead it is Yahweh who would build a *house* (dynasty) for David (7: 4-17). "And your house and your kingdom shall be made sure for ever before me; your throne shall be established forever" (7: 16). In a long and moving prayer (7: 18-29) David thanks the Lord. He starts on a personal note:

> Who am I, O Lord God, and what is my house, that thou hast brought me thus far? And yet this was a small thing in thy eyes, O Lord God; thou hast spoken also of thy servant's house for a great while to come, and hast shown me future generations, O Lord God! And what more can David say to thee? For thou knowest thy servant, O Lord God! (7: 18-20)

David goes on to outline God's matchless greatness, and his goodness to his people Israel and to David himself. And he concludes:

> And now, O Lord God, thou art God, and thy words are true, and thou hast promised this good thing to thy servant; now therefore may it please thee to bless the house of

thy servant, that it may continue forever before thee; for
thou, O Lord God, hast spoken, and with thy blessing shall
the house of thy servant be blessed forever (7: 28-29).

Before long we are sharply reminded of the sheer humanness of David. He, too, can compound a crime by an attempt at a cover-up. It is clear that his adultery with
Bathsheba was an open secret; her husband Uriah was
quite aware that he had been cuckolded (11: 1-13). David's
next move is wholly unworthy of one who before, and
again, displays greatness—he engineered the death of
Uriah (11: 12-25). It is cold-blooded murder. The only
redeeming feature is that, when challenged by a prophet,
David acknowledged his double sin (12: 1-15). We may not
fully appreciate the enormous significance of the episode.
After all, David was undisputed master: king of Judah and
Israel, and a petty emperor to boot. In any other society of
the time, he might have had any woman of his desire for
the taking. But, in the setting of Yahwism, the king too
was subject to the law of his God. David had to resort to
murder if he would have the wife of another (his subject).
In a different setting, a prophet would not have so brazen-
ly challenged his king, as Nathan did, and kept his head.
More surprisingly, the prophet obviously expected the confession and the repentance of his king. Truly, Yahweh is
not like other gods. Not even the king may flout his law.
And it is to David's credit that he sees it so. He makes no
excuses. The sequel shows him free once more of his
disastrous aberration and measuring up to the stature that
is truly his.

This we see in the marvelously vivid narrative of 12:
15-23—David's prayer for his stricken child, the child of
his adultery with Bathsheba. Here we have the gifted
author of the Court History of David (2 Sam 9-20; 1 Kgs
1-2) at his brilliant best. Commentary would be an imper-
tinence.

> And the Lord struck the child that Uriah's wife bore to
> David, and it became sick. David therefore besought God

for the child; and David fasted and went in and lay all night upon the ground. And the elders of his house stood beside him, to raise him from the ground; but he would not, nor did he eat food with them. On the seventh day the child died. And the servants of David feared to tell him that the child was dead; for they said, "Behold, while the child was yet alive, we spoke to him, and he did not listen to us; how then can we say to him the child is dead? He may do himself some harm?" But when David saw that his servants were whispering together, David perceived that the child was dead; and David said to his servants: "Is the child dead?" They said, "He is dead." Then David arose from the earth, and washed, and anointed himself, and changed his clothes; and he went into the house of the Lord, and worshipped; he then went to his own house; and when he asked, they set food before him, and he ate. Then his servants said to him, "What is this thing that you have done? You fasted and wept for the child while it was alive; but when the child died, you arose and ate food?" He said, "While the child was still alive, I fasted and wept, for I said, 'Who knows whether the Lord will be gracious to me, that the child may live?' But now he is dead; why should I fast? Can I bring him back again? I shall go to him, but he will not return to me" (12: 15-23).

It is surely David's finest hour.

David had confessed and repented, but he had sown his dragon's teeth; he must reap the harvest of bitter family strife. This great king turns out to be a comforting biblical hero: for all his greatness he is flesh and blood and has his times of weakness and of failure. We have seen something of that weakness; we learn that the gifted statesman who could achieve and maintain the unity of two kingdoms (Judah and Israel) was a disaster as a family man. He had spoiled his sons and had paid the price. He barely escaped not replacement only but death as well at the hand of his favorite, the arrogant Absalom (13: 1-19: 8). And, at the close of his days, his own plans for the succession were almost circumvented by another ambitious son, Adonijah (1 Kgs 1).

It seems that it took disaster to bring out again the best in David. While he fled before the forces of Absalom he was grossly insulted by Shimei, a Benjaminite and supporter of Saul's family who resented David's kingship (2 Sam 16: 5-7). David's officers wanted to take appropriate action—"Let me go over and take off his head," pleaded the general Abiskai (16:9). But David will have none of it:

> Behold, my own son seeks my life; how much more may this Benjaminite! Let him alone, and let him curse; for the Lord has bidden him. It may be that the Lord will look upon my affliction, and that the Lord will repay me with good for this cursing of me today (16: 11-12).

Here is a David tried and mellowed by adversity—a far cry from the touchy younger David who would have wiped out Nabal and his family, simply because the man was a boor (1 Sam 25: 1-13, 34).

We take our leave of David the scarred warrior and marred follower of Yahweh. The verdict of Hamlet on his father is appropriate: "He was a man, take him for all in all..." This lusty and vulnerable David of 2 Samuel is so much more congenial than the "saint" of 1 Chronicles. We did not have to await the Christian era to meet our hagiographers. Surely, we must find more encouragement in the flawed hero of 2 Samuel than in the white-power knight of 1 Chronicles.

1, 2 KINGS

When we move into 1 Kings we meet with Solomon. As we judge him today we can see, readily enough, that, for all his grandiose style—little short of megalomania—he is only a pale shadow of his father. But he did become the proverbial man of wisdom. And, for whatever reason, we have more prayer attributed to him than to any other.

At his first appearance, Solomon is one wholly pleasing to the Lord. He displays a touching gratitude to God for the grace of kingship:

> And now, O Lord my God, thou hast made thy servant
> king in place of David my father, although I am but a little
> child. [A little child born with a silver spoon in his mouth,
> and that does make a difference!] I do not know how to go
> out or come in [i.e., how to lead my people]. And thy ser-
> vant is in the midst of thy people whom thou hast chosen, a
> great people that cannot be numbered or counted for
> multitude. Give thy servant therefore an understanding
> mind to govern thy people, that I may discern between
> good and evil (1 Kgs 3: 7-9).

Solomon had been invited to request whatever gift he
wished (3:5) and had asked for wisdom, much to the
delight of the Lord (3:10-14). The tragedy is that the
graced Solomon cannot live up to his promise and his endowment. He started off with everything going for him,
but it is David and not Solomon who caught biblical im-
agination and holds the interest of Christians. Yet, when it
comes to prayer, Solomon has the edge. He was the man
who had built the temple envisaged by David (1 Kgs 5-7).
Solomon is the king-priest who officiated at the dedication
of the temple he had built. Naturally, such a liturgical occasion called for a suitably elaborate prayer. And Solomon
rose to the occasion. In authentically high-priestly fashion
(the high priest, on the Day of Expiation, first sacrificed
for himself, Lev 16:6), Solomon first prays for himself (1
Kgs 8: 23-26). Then he prays for his people, that the temple
may be their place of efficacious supplication: if a man sins
against his neighbor—if the people suffer defect—if there
is a disastrous drought—if there be famine: in all cases the
suppliants will find a ready hearing. Even the foreign so-
journer will be received (1 Kgs 8: 31-43).

One must appreciate that we are here dealing with the
deuteronomical history, and that means one must allow
for the trauma of the Exile. In this prayer the passage, vv
46-51, refers to that tragic situation, long after the age of
Solomon. It rings with an optimism that is typical of the
faith of Israel.

If they sin against thee—for there is no man who does not
sin [cf 1 Jn 1:8-2:2]—and thou art angry with them and
dost give them to an enemy, so that they are carried away
captive to the land of the enemy, far off or near; yet if they
lay it to heart in the land to which they have been carried
captive, and repent, and make supplication to thee in the
land of their captors, saying, "We have sinned, and have
acted perversely and wickedly"; if they repent with all their
mind and with all their heart in the land of their enemies,
who carried them captive, and pray to thee toward their
land, which thou gavest to their fathers, the city which
thou hast chosen, and the house which I have built for thy
name; then hear thou in heaven thy dwelling place their
prayer and their supplication, and maintain their cause and
forgive thy people who have sinned against thee, and all
their transgressions which they have committed against
thee; and grant them compassion in the sight of those who
carried them captive, that they may have compassion on
them (1 Kgs 8: 46-50).

That prayer of Solomon ends with a solemn blessing, one
that is truly moving:

The Lord our God be with us, as he was with our fathers;
may he not leave us or forsake us; that he may incline our
hearts to him, to walk in all his ways, and to keep his commandments, his statutes, and his ordinances which he commanded our fathers. Let these words of mine, wherewith I
have made supplication before the Lord, be near to the
Lord our God day and night, and may he maintain the
cause of his servant, and the cause of his people Israel, as
each day requires; that all the peoples of the earth may
know that the Lord is God; there is no other. Let your
heart therefore be wholly true to the Lord our God, walking in his statutes and keeping his commandments, as at
this day (8: 57-61).

This prayer of Solomon merits a reply from Yahweh
(9:1-9), a reply based on the deuteronomical doctrine of
the "two ways"—the way of faithfulness to Yahweh or the
way of disobedience (cf Dt 30: 15-20):

If you will walk before me, as David your father walked, with integrity of heart and uprighteousness, doing according to all that I have commanded you, and keeping my statutes and my ordinances, then I will establish your royal throne over Israel forever, as I promised David your father. . . But if you turn aside from following me, you or your children, and do not keep my commandments and my statutes which I have set before you, but go and serve other gods and worship them, then I will cut off Israel from the land which I have given them; and the house which I have consecrated for my name I will cast out of my sight; and Israel will become a proverb and a byword among all peoples (9: 4-5, 6-7).

Hezekiah

When King Hezekiah had received Sennacherib's peremptory demand for surrender (2 Kgs 19: 9-13) he went to the temple, spread out the Assyrian king's letter before the Lord (8: 14) and reminded Yahweh that he owed it to himself to humble the Assyrian's arrogance (19: 15-19). He ends with the plea:

So now, O Lord our God, save us, I beseech thee, from his hand, that all the kingdoms of the earth may know that thou, O God, art God alone (19:19).

The prophet Isaiah is sent to Hezekiah to assure him that his prayer has been heard (19: 20-34). "And that night the angel of the Lord went forth, and slew a hundred and eighty-five thousand in the camp of the Assyrians. . . Then Sennacherib, king of Assyria, departed. . . " (19:35-36). In other words, an epidemic decimated the Assyrian forces (the numbers, typically in such narratives, are grossly exaggerated). One must at least acknowledge that the timing was right and Jerusalem did not fall. In 2 Chronicles (32: 20-21) the deliverance is attributed to the prayer of "Hezekiah the king and Isaiah the prophet." Hezekiah had played, manfully, the role of intercessor for his people. He can also plead for himself. Struck by an illness that promises to be fatal (20:1),

> Hezekiah turned his face to the wall and prayed to the Lord, saying, "Remember now, O Lord, I beseech thee, how I have walked before thee in faithfulness and with a whole heart, and have done what is good in thy sight" (20:2-3).

His fervent prayer was answered; and, again, Isaiah is the bearer of good tidings (20: 5-6).

1, 2 CHRONICLES

The debt of the Chronicler to Samuel-Kings is patent: these earlier writings are his main sources. His primary purpose is to write a history of the dynasty of David, to bring out what it achieved in the religious sphere, especially in matters of cult, and to establish legitimate patterns of institutions and their personnel for the people of God. The Chronicler built his history and theology around these fundamental points. His work is a history, and a theology of history, quite different from that of the deuteronomists. Given the specific interest in matters cultic, we not only hear again prayers of David and Solomon, but more of these and in more elaborate guise.

The first prayer of David we come across, on the occasion of the bringing of the ark to Jerusalem, seems to be a collage of parts of Pss 105, 96, and 106. It is a hymn of praise. Next, while the prayer of David when he had been assured by Nathan that the Lord had built him a house is almost word-for-word the same as in 2 Samuel (1 Chr 17: 1-27; 2 Sam 7: 18-29), it is remarkable that the prayer appears in Chronicles at all given the fact that this work is post-exilic (about 300 B.C.), for the house of David had, historically, ended centuries earlier. The repetition of the prayer here points to a re-interpretation, in a more directly messianic direction, of the promise made to David.

The Chronicler passes over in silence David's adultery with Bathsheba and his murder of her husband. On the other hand, he develops the episode of 2 Samuel 24. David (in 1 Chr 21:1 instigated by Satan—the Accuser) had dared to take a census of *God's* people; this was tantamount to declaring them to be *his* people. "God was displeased with this thing" (1 Chr 21:7). As before (2 Sam 12: 1-13) David acknowledged his sin and repented of it (1 Chr 21: 8). He is offered three choices: three years of famine in the land; or three months as a fugitive before his enemies; or three days of the sword of the Lord (pestilence) (21: 11-12). David considers only choices two and three and has no hesitation in deciding between them: "Let me fall into the hand of the Lord, for his mercy is very great; but let me not fall into the hand of man" (21: 13). His final plea, when the pestilence had struck, makes clear that the first choice, a lengthy famine in the land, was never a serious choice for him.

> Was it not I who gave command to number the people? It is I who have sinned and done very wickedly. But these sheep, what have they done? Let thy hand, I pray thee, O Lord my God, be against me and against my father's house; but let not the plague be upon thy people (1 Chr 21: 17).

The Chronicler, who has so fulsomely idealized David, cannot quite hide the thorough humanness of the man. David is not only a sinner—he manfully acknowledges his sin. And he takes responsibility for the consequence of his sin and does not try to shift the blame. Not all the moments of his lust, and ruthlessness, and weakness, so mercilessly exposed in 2 Samuel, can outweigh the basic honesty and courage and fidelity of the man. He did, faithfully, serve his people and his God. David's special place in religious history is richly deserved.

It is quite in keeping with the Chronicler's picture of him that David's last appearance should be as high priest offering prayer for his people and their new king. His last prayer deserves to be quoted in full because it sounds just right on the lips of a David who had learned, over the years, to appreciate the privilege and the cost of serving the Lord.

> Therefore David blessed the Lord in the presence of all the assembly; and David said: "Blessed are thou, O Lord, the God of Israel our father, for ever and ever. Thine, O Lord, is the greatness, and the power, and the glory, and the victory, and the majesty; for all that is in the heaven and the earth is thine; thine is the kingdom, O Lord, and thou art exalted as head above all. Both riches and honor come from thee, and thou rulest over all. In thy hand are power and might; and in thy hand it is to make great and to give strength to all. And now we thank thee, our God, and praise thy glorious name.

> But who am I, and what is my people, that we should be able thus to offer willingly? For all things come from thee, and of thy own have we given thee. For we are strangers before thee, and sojourners, as all our fathers were; our days on the earth are like a shadow, and there is no abiding. O Lord our God, all this abundance that we have provided for building thee a house for thy holy name comes from thy hand and is all thy own. I know, my God, that thou triest the heart, and hast pleasure in uprightness; in the uprightness of my heart I have freely offered all these things; and now I have seen thy people, who are present here, offering freely and joyously to thee. O Lord, the God of Abraham, Isaac, and Israel, our fathers, keep forever such purposes and thoughts in the hearts of thy people, and direct their hearts toward thee. Grant to Solomon my son that with a whole heart he may keep thy commandments, thy testimonies, and thy statutes, performing all, and that he may build the palace for which I have made provision" (1 Chr 29: 10-19).

In 2 Chronicles, predictably, the cultic role of Solomon is stressed. Surprisingly, the long prayer of Solomon, on the occasion of the dedication of the temple, is rather more solemn in 1 Kings 8: 22-53 than in 2 Chronicles 6: 12-42. On second thought, it is not really surprising at all, given the avowed purpose of the Chronicler to upstage the cultic role of David. Perhaps a main difference lies in the setting of the prayer and in the king's posture. In 1 Kings 8: 22 Solomon "stood before the altar of the Lord in the presence of all the assembly of Israel, and spread forth his hands towards heaven." But in 2 Chronicles 6: 13, after that same statement had been quoted, there is the addition: "Solomon had made a platform five cubits long, five cubits wide, and three cubits high, and had set it in the court; and he stood upon it. Then he knelt upon his knees in the presence of all the assembly of Israel, and spread forth his hands towards heaven." This detail adds to the impressiveness of the scene.

The gist of Solomon's prayer re-emerges as a prayer of Jehoshaphat in 2 Chronicles 20: 6-12. According to 2 Chronicles 30, Hezekiah invited even inhabitants of former Israel to a solemn passover celebration. An interesting feature is that many who had eaten the passover, though they were ritually unclean, were cleansed, not by any ceremonial rite, but by a prayer of Hezekiah:

> For Hezekiah had prayed for them, saying, "The good Lord pardon every one who sets his heart to seek God, the Lord the God of his fathers, even though not according to the sanctuary's rules of cleanness" (30: 18-19).

The Chronicler alone tells of Manasseh's conversion and makes reference to his prayer of repentance (33: 10-19). A fruit of this reference is the apocryphal Prayer of Manasseh. It is a worthy example of post-exilic piety, a prayer of repentance more moving than the *Miserere*, and a salutary reminder that the Old Testament by no means represents the whole of the religious literature of Israel. For the simple, but adequate, reason that it may so readily be overlooked, it is thought well to give that prayer here:

O Lord Almighty,
  God of our fathers,
of Abraham and Isaac and Jacob
and of their righteous posterity;
thou who hast made heaven and earth
with all their order;
who hast shackled the sea by the word of command,
who hast confined the deep
and sealed it with thy terrible and glorious name;
at whom all things shudder,
and tremble before thy power,
for thy glorious splendor cannot be borne,
and the wrath of thy threat to sinners is irresistible;
yet immeasurable and unsearchable is thy promised mercy,
for thou art the Lord Most High,
of great compassion, long-suffering, and very merciful,
and repentest over the evils of men.
Thou, O Lord, according to thy great goodness
hast promised repentance and forgiveness
to those who have sinned against thee;
and in the multitude of thy mercies
thou hast appointed repentance for sinners,
that they may be saved,
Therefore thou, O Lord, God of the righteous,
hast not appointed repentance for the righteous,
for Abraham and Isaac and Jacob,
who did not sin against thee,
but thou hast appointed repentance for me, who am a
    sinner
For the sins I have committed are more in number than the
    sand of the sea;
my transgressions are multiplied,
O Lord, they are multiplied!
I am unworthy to look up and see the height of heaven
because of the multitude of my iniquities.
I am weighed down with many an iron fetter,
so that I am rejected because of my sins,
and I have no relief;
for I have provoked thy wrath
and have done what is evil in thy sight,
setting up abominations and multiplying offenses.
And now I bend the knee of my heart,

> beseeching thee for thy kindness.
> I have sinned, O Lord, I have sinned,
> and I know my transgressions.
> I earnestly beseech thee,
> forgive me, O Lord, forgive me!
> Do not destroy me with my transgressions!
> Do not be angry with me forever or lay up evil for me;
> do not condemn me to the depths of the earth.
> For thou, O Lord, art the God of those who repent,
> and in me thou wilt manifest thy goodness;
> for, unworthy as I am, thou wilt save me in thy great
>   mercy,
> and I will praise thee continually all the days of my life.
> For all the host of heaven sings thy praise,
> and thine is the glory forever. Amen.

If even *Manasseh* (cf 2 Kgs 21: 1-18, 2 Chr 33: 1-9) could, having turned back to the Lord, feel confident of salvation, there is hope for any and every sinner!

1,2 MACCABEES

Finally, we turn to the books of the Maccabees. We ought not be surprised to find a prayer of Judas, at the onset of battle (1 Mac 4: 30-33) couched in familiar terms; the author of 1 Maccabees has consciously imitated the style of Samuel and Kings. More numerous and interesting are the prayers in 2 Maccabees, a book written in a quite different literary style (and in Greek, not Hebrew). These prayers show us pharisaic judaism—or what came to be pharisaic judaism—at its best.

An important feature of 2 Maccabees is its confident teaching on the afterlife. We learn that the living may pray for the dead and make sin-offerings on their behalf.

> The noble Judas took up a collection, man by man, to the amount of two thousand drachmas of silver, and sent it to Jerusalem to provide for a sin offering. In doing this he acted very well and honorably, taking account of the resur-

rection. For if he were not expecting that those who had fallen would rise again, it would have been superfluous and foolish to pray for the dead. But if he was looking to the splendid reward that is laid up for those who fall asleep in godliness, it was a holy and pious thought. Therefore he made atonement for the dead, that they might be delivered from their sin (2 Mac 12: 43-45).

On the other hand, the just who have passed beyond the grave can intercede for those who still live on this earth. At a crucial phase of his military campaign, Judas Maccabeus was granted a vision:

What he saw was this: Onias, who had been high priest, a noble and good man, of modest bearing and gentle manner, one who spoke fittingly and had been trained from childhood in all that belongs to excellence, was praying with outstretched hands for the whole body of the Jews. Then likewise a man appeared, distinguished by his gray hair and dignity, and of marvelous majesty and authority. And Onias spoke, saying, "This is a man who loves the brethren and prays much for the people and the holy city, Jeremiah, the prophet of God." Jeremiah stretched out his right hand and gave to Judas a golden sword, and as he gave it he addressed him thus: "Take this holy sword, a gift from God, with which you will strike down your adversaries" (15: 12-16).

Here we have, for the first time explicitly stated, the doctrine of the communion of saints.

Judas remains the hero of the author of 2 Maccabees. Facing the threat of Antiochus IV, Judas bolstered his role of intercessor by getting his whole people involved in committed intercession to the Lord (13: 10-12). It is fitting that he should have the last prayer in the book. Facing the vastly superior forces of Nicanor, he prayed:

O Lord, thou didst send thy angel in the time of Hezekiah, king of Judea, and he slew a hundred and eighty-five thousand in the camp of Sennacherib. So now, O Sovereign of the heavens, send a good angel to carry terror and trembling before us. By the might of thy arm may these blasphemers who come against thy holy people be struck down. . .

Judas and his men met the enemy in battle with invocation to God and prayers. So, fighting with their hands and praying to God in their hearts, they laid low no less than thirty-five thousand men, and were greatly gladdened by God's manifestation (15: 22-24, 26-27).

This confident faith is admirable. It would be cruelly unfair to look at this picture of Judas through New Testament glasses. What does disturb is that Christians can so readily make that prayer of Judas their own—forgetting the uncomfortable but unmistakable teaching of *their* Lord: "love your enemy." One must admire the faith, the dedication, the sheer heroism of Old Testament servants of God. In so many ways they are so much nobler than we. But in this respect we may not follow them. Our Lord has shown us a way of peace.

Three

Prayer of the Prophets

Israel had its kings and its priesthood. And it had its bold critics of priests and people. It might be true to say that Yahweh had his fearless champions. The great prophets are men of stature, religious giants. Ahab had called Elijah a "troubler of Israel" and such, in his way, was every prophet. They were men who listened for the word of God and heard it; men who spoke the word, fearlessly, without counting the cost.

We had tended to speak of "greater" and "lesser" prophets—an arbitrary designation based on the comparative length of the prophetical books. By any standard "lesser" prophets like Amos and Hosea are major religious figures. "Isaiah" is more a prophetic school, ranging over several centuries. The strange imagery of Ezekiel marks a transition towards apocalyptic—as exemplified in the book of Daniel. For our purpose, the most interesting of the prophets is Jeremiah. He flourished in the last years of Judah, in the hopeful days of the young reformer, Josiah, but mostly in the years after that king's tragic death when Judah went, hell-bent, to its doom. In Jeremiah we can measure the greatness of a faithful servant of the word and learn of the price he must be prepared to pay.

It is to be expected that the prophets of Israel had made their contribution to the prayer of Israel. In one of them —Jeremiah—we reach a peak of prayer. But we cannot reasonably expect to find here many actual prayers. In the prophetic books it is generally God who speaks to man rather than the other way about.

ISAIAH and MICAH

Thanksgiving is a marked feature of Israel's prayer. And in Isaiah chapters 12 and 25 we find two typical hymns of thanksgiving:

> I will give thanks to thee, O Lord,
> for though thou was angry with me,
> thy anger turned away,
> and thou didst comfort me.
> Behold, God is my salvation;
> I will trust, and will not be afraid;
> for the Lord God is my strength and my song
> and he has become my salvation (12: 1-2).

> O Lord, thou art my God;
> I will exalt thee, I will praise thy name;
> for thou hast done wonderful things,
> plans formed of old, faithful and sure. . .
> For thou hast been a stronghold to the poor,
> a stronghold to the needy in his distress,
> a shelter from the storm and a shade from the heat
>   (25: 1, 4).

These psalms—for that is what they are—would be quite at home in the Psalter.

Now for some relevant snippets. A phrase from a song of victory (26: 1-6) is strikingly beautiful:

> Thou dost keep him in perfect peace, whose mind is stayed on thee, because he trusts in thee (26: 3).

And peace figures again in the subsequent hymn (26: 7-19):

> O Lord, thou wilt ordain peace for us, thou hast wrought
> for us all our works (26: 12).

In a psalm of hope in Yahweh (33: 1-6) there is the confident plea:

> O Lord, be gracious to us; we wait for thee. Be our arm
> every morning, our salvation in the time of trouble (33:2).

Isaiah, yet again, tells of Hezekiah's illness and deliverance (38: 1-8)—after all, the man was a *king*! But, unlike Kings and Chronicles, Isaiah goes on to give the text of the king's thanksgiving hymn (38: 10-29). One passage is of exceptional interest:

> Lo, it was for my welfare that I had great bitterness; for
> thou hast held back my life from the pit of destruction, for
> thou hast cast all my sins behind thy back (38: 17).

Implicit is the view that illness is occasioned by sin; that was, simply, the accepted position as we shall see in Job. What is remarkable here is a profound understanding of *divine* forgiveness. God had cast all of Hezekiah's sins behind his back, wholly out of his sight, never to be recalled again. This divine forgiveness is also finely expressed by Isaiah's contemporary, Micah:

> He does not retain his anger forever because he delights in
> steadfast love. He will again have compassion upon us, he
> will tread our iniquities under foot. Thou wilt cast all our
> sins into the depths of the sea (Micah 7: 18-19).

Together, these texts offer a penetrating and comforting theology of divine forgiveness. God will tread the sins of his repentant people deep into the ground, or will plunge them into the depths of the sea: he has buried them forever out of his sight. Divine forgiveness is absolute, with no strings attached. It is the forgiveness of the Prodigal Father

(Lk 15: 11-24). Nor is God's mercy confined to Israel: it reaches, also, to the Assyrian oppressor (cf Jonah 3: 5-10). This is something that the Israelite prophet, Jonah, cannot and will not accept (4: 2-3). His attitude, in one respect, is not unreasonable for he is being confronted with the injustice of God. Yes! the *injustice* of God! We glibly speak of God's justice. Well for us it is that God is radically unjust—by human standards. Paul, of course, realized this: "The proof of God's amazing love is that, while we were still sinners, Christ died for us, the ungodly" (Rom 5:6).

If we are to speak of "justice" here, then we have to acknowledge that God is a judge who acquits the guilty! To *acquit* a guilty man is blatant injustice. And we indignantly accuse some clever lawyers of manipulating the acquittal of the patently guilty. But God acquits the guilty all the time! We should rejoice at the injustice of our God. What is at issue, of course, is that God's justice, like his mercy, transcends our human categories. We have been exercised by the apparent conflict between God's sense of justice and his boundless mercy. Let us be satisfied that God has no such problem! Why *will* we persist in creating theological problems? David, we have seen, had the right idea when offered a choice:

> Let us fall into the hand of the Lord, for his mercy is great; but let us not fall into the hand of man (2 Sam 24: 14).

Better for us to trust to the foolish justice of the Lord than to the level-headed mercy of man.

HABAKKUK

In the prophet Habakkuk we meet with complaint— something that we shall find to be a characteristic of Jeremiah:

> O Lord, how long shall I cry for help, and thou wilt not hear? Or cry to thee "Violence!" and thou wilt not save?

> Why dost thou make me see wrongs and look upon trouble? (Hab 1: 2-3).

This text assures us that Jeremiah was not just being temperamental. Other prophets, too, could feel the burden of their office and be as candid in their complaining. But that is one facet only. We owe to Habakkuk a magnificent act of faith:

> Though the fig tree do not blossom,
> nor fruit be on the vines,
> the produce of the olive fail
> and the fields yield no food,
> the flock be cut off from the fold
> and there be no herd in the stalls,
> yet I will rejoice in the Lord,
> I will joy in the God of my salvation (3: 17-18).

JEREMIAH

Jeremiah, of all the prophets, is the best known to us. His book contains many passages of personal confession (where he opens his heart, like Augustine and Patrick), and autobiography, as well as lengthy sections of biography by his disciple and secretary, Baruch. In this, Jeremiah is quite like Paul. We are so fortunate in having not only Paul's own writing but a biography of Paul by Luke in his Acts of the Apostles. Jeremiah stands out as a lonely, tragic figure whose mission seemed to have failed. Yet, that "failure" was his triumph as later ages were to acknowledge.

It is possible to trace the spiritual progress of Jeremiah and to see in him the purifying and strengthening effect of suffering, for the most impressive message of the prophet was his own life. He was a man of rare sensitivity, with an exceptional capacity for affection—and his mission was "to pluck up and to break down, to destroy and to overcome" (1: 10).

At first, it seems, his mission was not so blatantly controversial. Like all the prophets, he was an intercessor, and what is, perhaps, his most beautiful prayer was spoken on occasion of a disastrous drought.

> Though our iniquities testify against us,
> act, O Lord, for thy name's sake;
> for our backslidings are many,
> we have sinned against thee.
> O thou hope of Israel,
> its savior in time of trouble,
> why shouldst thou be a stranger in the land,
> like a wayfarer who turns aside to tarry for a night?
> Why shouldst thou be like a man confused,
> like a mighty man who cannot save?
> Yet thou, O Lord, art in the midst of us,
> and we are called by thy name;
> leave us not (14: 7-9).

A beautiful prayer indeed and unmistakably, as we shall see, a prayer of Jeremiah. Is Yahweh nothing better than a stranger or a casual wayfarer?—is he a reluctant savior? This is Jeremiah all right! At the close, we find him still the intercessor (42: 1-4)—and that, too, is in character.

A grasp of the broad historical situation is essential for an understanding of Jeremiah. His mission was cast in the last days of the kingdom of Judah. Nebuchadnezzar and his Babylonian army were on the way. The people had a superstitious trust in the inviolability of Zion: Yahweh could never abandon his city and his temple. Their stance offers a good example of how one prophet might complicate matters for another. In the days of Sennacherib, a century before, Isaiah had confidently assured Hezekiah that, even though his kingdom had been overrun and he himself shut up in Jerusalem "like a bird in a cage" (as the Assyrian king put it), the city would not fall:

> Therefore thus says the Lord concerning the king of Assyria, He shall not come to this city or shoot an arrow there, or come before it with a shield or cast up a mound

against it. By the way he came, by the same he shall
return, and he shall not come into this city, says the Lord.
For I will defend this city to save it, for my own sake and
for the sake of my servant David. And that night the angel
of the Lord went forth and slew a hundred and eighty-five
thousand in the camp of the Assyrians (2 Kgs 19: 32-35;
Is 37: 33-36).

Jeremiah's contemporaries evidently expected a parallel
divine intervention in their day. Theirs was the sin of
presumption.

It was Jeremiah's task—and a hopeless one—to try to
bring his people to see that without a radical change of
heart, a genuine conversion, they were living in a fool's
paradise. The Babylonians were, in truth, God's judgment
on a grossly unfaithful people. Because there was not the
slightest hint that the people were going to change their
ways, Jeremiah has to insist that the nation is doomed. Not
surprisingly, this message was not popular with the govern-
ment. Jeremiah was regarded as a quisling and, more than
once, barely escaped with his life (cf 11:21; 18:18; 26: 7-19;
37: 11-21; 38: 1-13).

Most fascinating are the prophet's jousts with God. The
so-called Confessions (11: 18-12: 6; 15: 10-21; 17: 12-18;
18: 18-23; 20: 7-18) are central to an understanding of
Jeremiah. Not only are they fascinating because they per-
mit us to gaze into the heart of a prophet, they are above
all encouraging because they let us see how very human the
prophet is. Jeremiah had never really wanted to be a
prophet and he continued to discuss the trials of his office
with Yahweh throughout his life. He felt overwhelmed by
the sheer burden, the humanly impossible demands, of his
task. His prayer was the prayer of Gethsemane. Let us
look at some utterances of Jeremiah in his Confessions.

The Lord made it known to me and I knew; then you did
show me their evil deeds. But I was like a gentle lamb led to
the slaughter (11: 18-19).

While the prophet could clearly perceive the painful and tragic condition of the people, he has to learn that *he* is going to be dragged, as a victim, into their situation. A true prophet cannot be, in the Irish expression, "a hurler on the ditch"—he cannot stand aloof from the field of action.

> Your words were found, and I ate them, and your words became to me a joy and the delight of my heart; for I am called by your name, O Lord, God of hosts. I did not sit in the company of merrymakers, nor did I rejoice; I sat alone, because your hand was upon me. . . Why is my pain unceasing, my wound incurable, refusing to be healed? Will you be to me like a deceitful brook, like waters that fail? (15: 16-18; cf 14: 8-9).

This passage splendidly portrays both the privilege and the cost of vocation. As Ezekiel had also experienced, the prophetic word is bitter-sweet (Ezek 3: 1-3). Jeremiah's deep joy is that "I am called by your name"—he is a man of God. But this sets him apart; he cannot be as other men. He feels the lonely pang of his calling. His only companion is the Lord he serves—and will even he abandon him? This bitter cry from the heart wins a comforting response from Yahweh: "I will make you to this people a fortified wall of bronze; they will fight against you, but they shall not prevail over you, for I am with you to save you and deliver you, says the Lord" (15: 20).

> Heal me, O Lord, and I shall be healed; save me, and I shall be saved. Behold, they say to me, "What is the word of the Lord? Let it come!" I have not pressed you to send evil, nor have I desired the day of disaster—as you know. That which came out of my lips was your word (17: 14-16).

Again, the burden of the prophetic office. Jeremiah finds no pleasure in being a prophet of doom, does not enjoy being made the butt of sarcasm and sneer. He is doing no more than faithfully hearing and courageously proclaiming the word of the Lord. And he suffers because of his intense sympathy with the people over whom he must proclaim the

judgment of God. A brief prayer of Jeremiah puts his yet
more bitter utterances in perspective:

> I know, O Lord, that the way of man is not in himself, that
> it is not in man who walks to direct his steps. Correct me,
> O Lord, but in just measure; not in your anger, lest you
> bring me to nothing (10: 23-24).

By candidly acknowledging the moral and spiritual in-
capacity of man left to himself, Jeremiah admits that he,
too, must have failed. He looks with confidence, however,
to divine correction, knowing that it will be in due
measure. He is in no way inhibited by a prospect of
discipline.

> O Lord, you have deceived me, and I was deceived; you are
> stronger than I, and you have prevailed. I have become a
> laughingstock all the day; everyone mocks me (20: 7).

This is truly marvelous. Let us just look at what Jeremiah
implies when he declares: "you are stronger than I!" What
he says in effect is: "Yahweh, you are a great big bully!"
He has had it up to *here*. And he tells his God so in no
uncertain terms. There is something wonderfully
refreshing in this virile approach to God. For Jeremiah, his
God is so real, so personal, that he can speak out to him
with outrageous boldness. The decisive factor is that
Jeremiah can do so from a position of strength. He is a
prophet who, no matter how hard it went, was unflinch-
ingly faithful to the service his God had asked of him.

Jeremiah had come to his wit's end. He wanted to pack
it all in.

> If I say, "I will no longer mention him, or speak any more
> in his name," there is in my heart as it were a burning fire
> shut up in my bones, and I am weary with holding it in,
> and I cannot (20: 9).

While the prophet is doubtlessly thinking of the urgency of
the prophetic word his cry will find an echo in the heart of

any man or woman who serves the Lord in a painful situation. It is never easy to bear witness in the face of repulse. It is so much more difficult in the face of blank indifference. Why not just pack one's bags and slip away? Only a profound conviction of vocation can hold one to the task. It is comforting to know that even a Jeremiah could contemplate "changing his option!"

The Faithful Servant

It is against this background of demand and stress that one may gauge the greatness of Jeremiah. One is saddened by the word "jeremiad" and what it implies. Jeremiah had to strive to jolt his people into conversion. He was no grim prophet of doom. The truth of this is borne out dramatically in the later phase of his career. When Nebuchadnezzar had captured and destroyed Jerusalem (as Jeremiah had, for years, threatened that Nebuchadnezzar would do) did the prophet crow over it and shout out: "I told you so!" Far from it. The time for threats is over. Disaster has struck, and here is a shattered people. Jeremiah can teach many Christians a salutary lesson. One does not gloat over disaster nor see it as a vindication of one's cause. The service that God asks of his servants is to help and comfort the afflicted. And Jeremiah's tune changes, radically. There is no change in the prophet. He is still being God's faithful servant.

His service had been to try and bring his people to their senses. His service now is to comfort them in their bewilderment.

> Behold, the days are coming, says the Lord, when I will make a new covenant with the house of Judah. . . This is the covenant which I will make with the house of Israel after those days, says the Lord: I will put my law within them, and I will write it upon their hearts; and I will be their God, and they shall be my people (31: 31, 33).

His service had not been in vain. In the searing light of the disaster the people will come to see the truth of the faithful prophet's message. Jeremiah is the supreme example—until Jesus Christ—of the triumph of failure.

Hate Your Enemy

It would be less than honest to treat of Old Testament prayer and leave out of sight one disturbing aspect. Many of us, in our time, have had trouble with the "cursing psalms." What is one to make of the following where the psalmist solemnly curses his enemy?

> May his days be few;
> may another seize his goods!
> May his children be fatherless,
>   and his wife a widow!
> May his children wander about and beg;
>   may they be driven out of the ruins they inhabit!. . .
> Let there be none to extend kindness to him,
>   nor any to pity his fatherless children!. . .
> May the iniquity of his fathers be remembered before the
>   Lord,
>   and let not the sin of his mother be blotted out!
> (Ps 109: 8-14).

Pretty bloodthirsty indeed! And there are several comparable passages. Nor should we imagine that only the psalmists are guilty. Jeremiah can curse as vehemently as any of them. The prophet describes himself as "a gentle lamb led to the slaughter"—at the mercy of his enemies (Jer 11: 19). But now that he has discovered their designs, he begs: "let me see thy vengeance upon them" (11: 20)—not much of the "gentle lamb" there! What shape that vengeance should take, he spells out later.

He had pleaded before Yahweh for this people and they had repaid his solicitude with evil (18: 19-20). Very well, then, let them have their just deserts:

> Therefore deliver up their children to famine;
> give them over to the power of the sword,
> let their wives become childless and widowed.
> May their men meet death by pestilence,
> their youths be slain by the sword in battle. . .
> Forgive not their iniquity,
> nor blot out their sin from thy sight.
> Let them be overthrown before thee;
> deal with them in the time of thine anger (18: 21-23).

These are certainly not Christian sentiments. But why should they be? They are the sentiments of pre-Christian man. "Love your enemy" is a revolutionary doctrine of Jesus. We have no right to criticize religious men before the age of Jesus for failing to measure up to his ideal. What ought to concern us is that we Christians have failed to measure up to what he has asked of us. The Old Testament, while it is an integral part of our Christian scripture, is pre-Christian. There is no overlooking that fact; and there will always be some tension in our assimilation of the Old Testament. The remarkable fact is that we can relate to so much of it and can learn so very much from it. But such sentiments as we have just noted have no place in Christian prayer.

These passages remain, of course, part of the Old Testament and we should seek to understand them in their setting, even in their prayer-context. But we should not attempt to use them in *our* prayer. They simply will not fit into Christian prayer. Wisely, the new breviary has left such psalm-passages aside. This is the proper course, indeed the only course. It is consoling to note that in the psalter, as in Jeremiah and elsewhere, there is really so little of this (to us) jarring note. We ought to be thankful for the great positive contribution of Israel and, sensibly, set quietly aside what will no longer help us. That is why our reference to this cursing of enemies is little more than an explanatory footnote.

Four

Prayer of the Sages

The religion of the Old Testament (like that of the New Testament) is firmly historical. Israel came to know its God in the event of the Exodus when God entered into its history. A group of writings within the Old Testament, however, seem to abstract from history. They are concerned, in the main, with prudent and moral conduct (Proverbs; Sirach) but also with the deepest human problems (Job, Qoheleth). These varied writings are the work of the sages, the "wise men."

"Wisdom" was the love of the ancient world, long established in Egypt and Mesopotamia before it struck root in Israel. The sages were the literate men of the day, the civil servants in the political administration. As cultivated men, they could rise above the pragmatic and turn to what we would term philosophical speculation. In Israel the wise men, sincere Yahwists all of them, found themselves facing theological questions, as in Job and Qoheleth.

On another level, the sages could still make their mark. Baruch and Sirach find in the Torah, the Law, the sum of wisdom. The Song of Songs is fair comment on the Yahwist's ideal picture of man and woman (Genesis 2: 18-25) as it extols, with exuberance, the joys of love. The sophisticated Book of Wisdom is, in great part, a critique of Egyptian religion in the first century B.C. But Job will always be the measure of Israel's religious and poetic achievement.

Where the prophets of Israel were the men of the Spirit and of the Word, the sages were the men of Wisdom. But they, too, were first and foremost Yahwists. They were men of their time with a view of reality which we do not necessarily share. In the main part of the Book of Proverbs, for instance, we find what seems to us a disconcerting jumble of "secular" and "religious" proverbs and maxims. We would have arranged them neatly under those or similar headings. But such a distinction is ours—not that of the sages. For them, reality was one and the hand of God was to be discerned in all things. If human life had its own dimension, that too was from God.

Part of that human dimension was the search for knowledge. And, because there is one world of experience, in coming to grips with that world rational perceptions and religious perceptions were not differentiated. Israel did not keep faith and knowledge apart. In the wise men's search for knowledge, even when they expressed the results in a wholly secular form, there was never any question of what we might call "pure" knowledge functioning independently of their faith in Yahweh. This is brought out in a sentence which, in one form or another, occurs five times in the wisdom literature: "The fear of Yahweh is the beginning of knowledge" (Prov 1: 7; cf Prov 9: 10; 15: 33; Ps 111: 10; Job 28: 28).

We grasp the import of the saying when we realize that the phrase "fear of Yahweh" means knowledge of Yahweh or, better, commitment to Yahweh. The saying means, then, that the fear of God leads to wisdom. The sages believed, quite simply, that effective knowledge about God and a right relation with him is the only way to attain true knowledge. Faith does not hinder knowledge. Faith enabled one to see all things in right perspective and set one free to evaluate them properly. Wisdom stands or falls according to the right attitude of man to God.

The sages, then, are in no sense rationalists. Instead, they were men of faith, deeply religious. The opposite of the wise man is the "fool." The contrast "wise-foolish" (and not "wise-ignorant") is significant: even the highly skilled, cultured man is a "fool" if he has not grasped the true meaning and purpose of life. Folly is practical atheism: "The fool says in his heart, 'There is no God'" (Ps 14: 1).

For the sages, all human knowledge comes back to the question about commitment to God. They were, then, men of prayer. Oddly, we do not have many of their prayers. But we have something better. We have Job's struggle with his God. It is Jeremiah all over again, but now presented with consummate art by a poet-theologian. Before coming to that, we will look at Sirach, the Book of Wisdom and Tobit. There are no prayers in Proverbs, Qoheleth and the Song of Songs.

SIRACH

The first prayer in Sirach (36: 1-17) is typically post-exilic—it is a prayer for the deliverance and restoration of Jerusalem. It will be best to note it in our next chapter—it will be at home there. The section 39: 12-43: 33 of Sirach is a eulogy of the Lord in his governance of the universe. It opens with an invitation to praise God (39: 12-35) and closes with an elaborate hymn to the Lord (42: 15-43; 33).

The call is issued: "Bless the Lord for all his works" (39:14). The calm conviction is that everything in creation has its place and its purpose (cf v 21). Moreover:

> From the beginning good things were created for good people, just as evil things for sinners (v 25).

There are weapons of God's anger: winds, wild beasts, the sword (vv 28-31)—all are from the Lord.

The works of the Lord are all good, and he will supply every need in its hour. And no one can say, "This is worse than that," for all things will prove good in their season. So now sing praise with all your heart and voice, and bless the name of the Lord (vv 33-35).

The hymn (42:15-43:33) extols the glory of the Lord reflected in his works. In the first place there is the Lord's greatness in his creation as such (42: 15-33).

The sun looks down on everything with its light and the work of the Lord is full of his glory (42: 16).

His creation is marked by order and completeness:

All things are twofold, one opposite the other, and he has made nothing incomplete. One confirms the good things of the other, and who can have enough of beholding his glory? (42: 24-25).

In 43: 1-26 the most striking works are listed: sun, moon, stars, rainbow, snow, thunder, ice and the great deep. Particularly beautiful is the description of the rainbow:

Look upon the rainbow, and praise him who made it, exceedingly beautiful in its brightness. It encircles the heaven with its glorious arc; the hands of the Most High have stretched it out (43: 11-12).

In the conclusion (43: 27-33) the poet is quite carried away:

Though we speak much we cannot reach the end, and the sum of our words is: "He is the all." Where shall we find strength to praise him? For he is greater than all his works. . . When you praise the Lord, exalt him as much as you can; for he will surpass even that. When you exalt him, put forth all your strength, and do not grow weary, for you cannot praise him enough (43:27-30).

The hymn is manifestly inspired by the splendid story of creation in Genesis 1. And it builds on the assertion: "God saw everything that he had made, and behold, it was very good" (Gen 1: 31). It is the same conviction we find in the Book of Wisdom: "For from the greatness and beauty of created things comes a corresponding perception of their Creator" (Wis 13: 5). And in Paul: "For what can be known about God is plain to them, because God has shown it to them. Ever since the creation of the world his invisible nature, namely his eternal power and deity, has been clearly perceived in the things that have been made" (Rom 1: 19-20). Clearly, for Israel, nature pointed straight to God. And nature was a powerful inspiration of prayer.

A hymn of thanksgiving (Sirach 51: 1-12) is quite like the thanksgiving hymns of the psalter—the sage has been rescued from his enemies and thanks the God who has been his only savior. And Jesus ben Sirach leaves us with the assurance that his wisdom was a gift of God in answer to prayer:

> While I was still young, before I went on my travels, I sought wisdom openly in my prayer. Before the temple I asked for her and I will search for her to the last (51: 13-14).

THE BOOK OF WISDOM

The latest of the wisdom books, the Book of Wisdom, also has its appeal and its prayer for wisdom. Solomon—the first century B.C. author writes in the name of the famous king—firmly asserts that his renowned wisdom was purely answer to prayer:

> Therefore I prayed, and understanding was given me; I called upon God, and the spirit of wisdom came to me (Wis 7:7).

No doubt, this is inspired by the passage in 1 Kings 3: 3-14; cf 2 Chronicles 1: 3-13. The king goes on to pray that God

may grant him always to speak with judgment. And he
asserts: "it is he who gave me unerring knowledge of what
exists" (Wis 7:17). The speech of the king (7: 1-8: 21) concludes with a prayer for wisdom (9: 1-18).

> O God of my fathers and Lord of mercy. . .
> Give me the wisdom that sits by thy throne,
> and do not reject me from among thy servants. . .
> Send her forth from thy holy heavens,
> and from the throne of thy glory send her,
> that she may be with me and toil,
> and that I may learn what is pleasing to thee.
> Who has learned thy counsel, unless thou hast given
>   wisdom
> and sent thy holy Spirit from on high?
> And thus the paths of those on earth were set right
> and men were taught what pleases thee,
> and were saved by wisdom (9: 1, 4, 10, 17-18).

The final sentence is an adroit transition to the role of
wisdom in human affairs from Adam to the Exodus (10:
1-11:3). Sirach and Wisdom make quite clear that, for the
later sages at least, their wisdom endowment was an
answer to prayer.

TOBIT

The Book of Tobit is concerned with a double case of
the just sufferer. Tobit, a model of observance and of
charity, is the victim of an unfortunate accident. Sarah, an
innnocent girl, is grievously afflicted through no fault of
her own. Both become the butt of bitter tongues (Tob 2:
14; 3: 8) and, as a result, both seek to die (3: 7, 15). The
story raises two of the major problems faced by the
wisdom writers: Is virtue rewarded? Is life worth living?
The key to the book is found in Tobit 3: 16-17 and 12:
12-15. The prayer of the two unhappy ones is presented to
God by Raphael, and the angel is entrusted with a mission
to help them. Azarias (in other words, the angel Raphael in

human guise) is indeed the instrument of God's providence. He is a dramatic answer to prayer. This delightful
writing is pervaded by an atmosphere of faith and trust in
God, and of joyful thanksgiving. The story is, in its
fashion, an impressive treatise on prayer.

The first prayer in the book is Tobit's lament (Tob 3:
2-6). It takes for granted not only the view that sickness
and suffering are the consequence of personal sin (3: 3, 5),
but also the theory of solidarity: he is suffering, also, for
the sins of his fathers (3: 3, 5). This last is an outlook that
persisted, despite the rejection of it by Jeremiah and
Ezekiel (cf Jer 31: 29; Ezek 18). It even crops up in John 9:
1-2. Tobit's prayer is that he may die:

> And now deal with me according to thy pleasure; com-
> mand my spirit to be taken up, that I may depart and
> become dust. For it is better for me to die than to live,
> because I have heard false reproaches, and great is the sor-
> row within me. Command that I now be released from my
> distress to go to the eternal abode; do not turn thy face
> from me (Tob 3: 6).

The poignancy of the prayer can be gauged when one
realizes that "the eternal abode" is not our heaven but
Sheol—a place of gloom and a state of helpless inactivity
(cf Is 38: 18). Life had become too bitter for Tobit; he
wants nothing more than to go quietly and speedily to the
grave. Sarah (Tob 3: 11-15) prays in like manner—her
prayer we shall see later.

Noteworthy is the conclusion of the chapter, in which
the episodes of Tobit and Sarah are neatly linked:

> The prayer of both was heard in the presence of the glory
> of the great God. And Raphael was sent to heal the two of
> them. . . At that very moment Tobit returned and entered
> his house and Sarah the daughter of Raguel came down
> from her upper room (3: 16-17).

Raphael will later explain (12: 12, 15): "When you and
your daughter-in-law Sarah prayed, I brought a reminder

of your prayer before the Holy One. . . . I am Raphael, one of the seven holy angels who present the prayers of the saints and enter into the presence of the glory of the Holy One!" The angel had interceded for the suppliants and had been sent by God as the answer to their prayer. Here we have a preparation for the consoling teaching of the letter to the Hebrews. First, the assertion that angels are nothing other than "ministering spirits sent forth to serve, for the sake of those who are to obtain salvation" (Heb 1: 14). And then the assurance that it is no angel but our High Priest, the Son of God, who intercedes before God on our behalf (4: 15-16; 7: 25; 10: 19-22). Angels are expendable because we Christians have the Son as an advocate and the Spirit as the answer to our prayer (Lk 11: 13). Still, the story of Tobit remains an encouraging portrayal of intercession and response.

With superb skill, the author of Tobit traces the manner of God's response. Tobit (4: 1) recalled that he had, years before, entrusted a sum of money to his friend Gabael and he now decided to send his son Tobias to claim it. To be his son's companion and guide on the journey he hired a Jew named Azarias (the reader knows that he is, in fact, the angel Raphael—Ch 5). The angel encouraged the young man in face of danger, and aided him to procure remedies for his father's blindness, and against the machinations of evil spirits—thus he could deliver Sarah (6: 1-8). Moreover, he so effectively extolled the charms of Sarah that Tobias, before ever he had set eyes on the girl, "fell in love with her and lost his heart to her hopelessly" (6: 17). At Ecbatana they visited the home of Raguel. Tobias wasted no time in seeking Sarah's hand. Despite his apprehension (for Sarah had been betrothed seven times, and each time the evil demon Asmodeus had slain the unfortunate fiance) Raguel agreed. This time the demon was vanquished (7: 1-3).

The young couple were alone. Before they retired, Tobias spoke to his bride: "Sister, let us pray that the Lord may have mercy on us" (8: 4). This was in keeping with an admonishment of the angel: "When you approach her, rise up, both of you, and cry out to the merciful God, and he will save you and have mercy on you" (6: 17). Tobias prayed:

> Blessed are you, O God of our fathers,
> and blessed be your holy and glorious name forever.
> Let the heavens and all your creatures bless you.
> You made Adam and gave him Eve his wife
> as a helper and support.
> From them the race of mankind has sprung.
> You did say, "It is not good that the man should be alone;
> let us make a helper for him like himself."
> And now, O Lord, I am not taking this sister of mine
> because of lust, but with sincerity. Grant that I may find
> mercy and may grow old together with her.
> And she said with him, "Amen."
> Then they both went to sleep for the night (8: 5-9).

The prayer is manifestly inspired by Genesis 2: 7-24. Both texts reflect the positive, healthy attitude of Israel to sex and marriage. This becomes all the more clear when we compare the moralizing tone of the Vulgate version of Tobit. At 8:4 the Vulgate specifies that the prayer of the young couple lasted for three nights—and only then did the two sleep together. Already the Vulgate had spelled out its view (6: 18-22) in the angel's admonition to Tobias:

> When thou shalt take her, Sarah, into the chamber: and for three days keep thyself continent from her, and give thyself to nothing else but to prayers with her. . . And when the third night is past, thou shalt take the virgin with the fear of the Lord, moved rather for love of children than for lust: that in the seed of Abraham thou mayest obtain a blessing in children (6: 18, 22).

Obviously, these Vulgate prescriptions mark a grave departure from the serenity of the earlier story. The real Tobias echoes the inspiring and encouraging note of Genesis 2; the later additions sound an alien note. It is tragic that, in Christian history, it has had more resonance than the other.

In the meantime, Raguel could not hide his apprehension. He quietly dug a grave so that, if the worst happened, Tobias might be secretly buried before daylight (8:9). A maid sent to check found the young couple sleeping peacefully (8: 12-13) and Raguel gave vent to his relief in prayer:

> Blessed art thou, O God, with every pure and holy
>   blessing. . .
> Blessed art thou, because thou has had compassion on two
>   only children.
> Show them mercy, O Lord;
> and bring their lives to fulfilment in health and
> happiness and mercy (8: 15, 17).

After this, the story hastens to its close. When the elderly Tobit meets his son again and is cured of his blindness, his spontaneous reaction is thankful prayer:

> Blessed art thou, O God, and blessed is thy name forever, and blessed are all thy holy angels. For thou hast afflicted me, but thou hast had mercy upon me; here I see my son Tobias! (11:14-15).

Before taking his departure the angel addressed father and son and warmly recommended the traditional good works of prayer, fasting and almsgiving (12: 6-10). His emphasis is manifestly on prayer.

> Praise God and give thanks to him; exalt him and give thanks to him in the presence of all the living for what he has done for you. It is good to praise God and to exalt his name, worthily declaring the works of God. Do not be slow to give him thanks. . . Prayer is good when accompanied by fasting, almsgiving and righteousness (12: 6, 8).

JOB

With Job we arrive again at uninhibited boldness in approaching God. Here is a character worthy of the genius of his creator, the gifted and profound author of the Book of Job. Structurally, the work is an elaborate poem, framed by a prose prologue and epilogue. That prose setting is something much more than a naive story of the testing of Job (chs 1-2) and of the due reward of his fidelity (the final chapter)—all too good to be true. It is vitally important for an understanding of the great poem.

Twice, God himself bears witness to the uprightness of Job:

> Have you considered my servant Job, that there is none like him on the earth, a blameless and upright man, who fears God and turns away from evil? (1:8, cf 2:3).

Twice, Job himself comes through the test:

> In all this Job did not sin or charge God with wrong (1:22; cf 2:10).

And, of course, the last chapter, the restoration of Job's fortune, is, in fairy-tale style, his vindication. That older story is not incidental.

Job's Problem

The bulk of the book takes the shape of Job defending himself against his three friends. Without the prose setting we could never be sure who was in the right, he or they. But we, the readers, have been let into the secret. We know, what Job and his friends do not know, that Job *is* a righteous man, that he is in the right. Properly to understand Job's situation we must seek to understand his problem. Job wrestles with a tormenting problem: he is suffering, yet knows himself to be innocent. This was a situation which contradicted the accepted theological wisdom of the time which saw a close and necessary connection between suffering and sin. Here, the three friends are the champions of orthodoxy. They have accepted the standard doctrine without question and quite refuse to admit that it will not fit the facts of the present case. Their position is simple and straightforward: suffering is punishment of sin. If a man suffers it is because he is a sinner (for suffering, too, comes from God). This view lingered into New Testament times. Recall the question of the disciples, in John's gospel, when they came upon a blind man: "Rabbi, who sinned, this man or his parents, that he was born blind?" (Jn 9:1). Jesus, of course, rejects the implied view: "It was not that this man sinned or his parents. . ." (9:3). At the time of the book of Job—written about the end of the fifth century B.C.—it was taken for granted that suffering was occasioned by sin, and that it was punishment of sin. That is why the friends here try to bring Job to acknowledge that he is a sinner—and a mighty sinner at that, judging from his sufferings—and they grow more insistent as he protests his innocence.

Job's Prayer

Our concern is not primarily with Job's problem but rather with Job's prayer. In chapters 9 and 10 he asks, in radical fashion, whether man can argue with God. He paints the greatness of God, creator and master of all. What chance has mere man?

> If it is a contest of strength, behold him (Job 9:19).
> There is no umpire between us,
> who might lay his hand upon us both (9:33).

Yet, Job will not be put off:

> I will give free utterance to my complaint;
> I will speak in the bitterness of my soul.

> I will say to God, Do not condemn me;
> let me know why thou dost contend against me (10: 1-2).

The rest of the chapter is an anguished prayer. Wracked by
torments of body and of mind, suffering he does not
understand, he pleads for respite (10:20). But his God has
become his enemy:

> Know then that God has put me in the wrong,
> and closed his net about me. . .
> He has walled up my way, so that I cannot pass,
> and he has set darkness upon my paths. . .
> He has kindled his wrath against me,
> and counts me as his enemy (19: 6, 8, 11).

There is a deeper dimension still to Job's agony. He had
cried out to God and had yearned to meet him:

> I would speak to the Almighty,
> and I desire to argue my case with God (13:3).

But there is no answer. The accessible God of his former
days has now hidden his face and is silent. Job is immersed
in what Christian mystics have called a "dark night of the
soul." What he wants to know is. . . Why? Why has God
broken off their friendship? If only Job had a chance to
plead his case, then *his* God would quickly make all well
again.

> Oh, that I knew where I might find him,
> that I might come even to his seat!
> I would lay my case before him
> and fill my mouth with arguments. . .
> Would he contend with me in the greatness of his power?
> No; he would give heed to me.
> There an upright man could reason with him,
> and I should be acquitted forever by my judge (23: 3-7).

And he goes on, in the most poignant, and most beautiful,
passage in the book:

> Behold, I go forward, but he is not there;
> and backward, but I cannot perceive him;
> On the left hand I seek him, but I cannot behold him;
> I turn to the right hand, but I cannot see him.
> But he knows the way that I take;
> when he has tried me I shall come forth as gold (23: 8-10).

Job's Faith

What is one to do in face of such faith? Job will not be turned from a God who has become a stranger. Somewhere there must be an answer to this cruel riddle. He will learn that the answer is—as it alone must be—God himself. Strangely, as it seems, the shattering presumption of God's injustice and unfeelingness (24: 1-12) follows on Job's conviction of God's fairness and concern. This is the fluctuation of one who is being tried beyond endurance. What matters is that Job, at the bitter end, clings to his faith in *his* God who must stand behind that terrifying mask. At the close of his apologia he is still manfully pleading for an audience:

> Oh, that I had one to hear me!
> I have had my say! Now let the Almighty answer me!
> Oh, that I had the indictment written by my adversary!
> Surely I would carry it on my shoulder;
> I would bind it on me as a crown;
> I would give him an account of all my steps;
> like a prince I would approach him (31: 35-37).

Job has uttered his challenge and, fittingly, at the end, God does speak to him (chs 38-39). The dramatic theophany is now preceded by a long hymn in praise of God's wisdom and omnipotence (36: 22-37: 24) by Elihu—who, at a later date, had been introduced into the poem. Job has found again his God, he has found peace in the meeting.

> I had heard of thee by the hearing of the ear,
> but now my eye sees thee;

> therefore I despise myself,
> and repent in dust and ashes (42: 5-6).

Where Job had been at fault was in having tried to interfere in God's affairs. He had been right all along in his conviction that he needed only to find his God again for all to be well.

Though, however, he speaks of having seen God, the mystery remains. God's ways toward him are still inscrutable. But if theoretically the problem looms as large as ever, he has solved it as a practical issue: he has come to accept God as he is and he no longer questions the divine purpose. Hence, though we have shattered the stained-glass Job—the inhumanly patient man—we have raised, instead, the real Job, the man of faith. And from him we can learn that faith in a God whose ways we cannot know does lead to patience and to peace.

Five

Prayer of the Chastened

What is an Israelite to think or to say when God's solemn promise to Abraham and his word of assurance to David had come to naught? There was no questioning the harsh reality of Nebuchadnezzar's conquest: temple, city, and nation were gone. On the strength of Yahweh's word it ought not have been so; but it had happened. For the faithful Yahwist the disaster was a mirror held up before the nation, a mirror which showed a visage of gross failure and of sin. Failure indeed—but of the people of God, and not of God's word.

The faith-answer to the disasters was repentance and hope. The moving prayers of the exiled candidly confess sin. Their lengthy catalogue of Yahweh's benefits mercilessly outlines the ingratitude in recrimination. From the clash of generosity and thanklessness leaps a spark of hope, a spark that is blown into a steady flame. The Lord will listen to the prayer of the chastened ones. . . because the Lord has heard. A faithful God stands waiting for a return.

> The Lord did not turn from the fierceness of his great anger which was kindled against Judah. . . And the Lord said: "I will remove Judah also out of my sight, as I have removed Israel, and the Temple of which I have said: My Name shall be there" (2 Kgs 23: 26-27).

For men of faith it was self-evident: Yahweh—with good reason—was angry with his people. This was the only acceptable explanation of the traumatic disaster of the Exile. Jeremiah had been proved right. The house built by Abraham and Moses and David had crashed in ruins. But the situation was not hopeless. The people had failed—of that there could be no doubt. But Yahweh was as steadfast and faithful as ever. There was a way of restoration, a way of redemption. It was the way of candid confession of sin, and of total trust in God's boundless mercy. While post-exilic prayers tend to be lengthy, there is about them a refreshing candor and an inspiring faith. They are the prayers of a chastened people, a people that, in adversity, had found its soul. Perhaps nothing as much as these prayers illustrates the ennobling influence of the religion of Yahweh. Those who pray them do not grovel; they maintain a quiet dignity. They are prayers truly worthy of the God to whom they are addressed and of the people of God who pray.

LAMENTATIONS and BARUCH

Though traditionally attached to the book of Jeremiah (not, however, in the Hebrew Bible) *Lamentations* is not the work of the prophet. These poems (five, if one includes the "Prayer of Jeremiah") are laments for a fallen Jerusalem and ruined temple, composed by some who had been left in Judah after the disaster, and designed for a simple liturgical service in the ruins of the temple. Through them runs a sentiment of unshaken trust in God and an air of deep repentance. They prepare for the message of Jesus that repentance is joy: a coming home to a Father. They are at home in our Christian liturgy of Holy Week.

Characteristic of all these prayers is confession of sin. Yet, if there is the admission that "Jerusalem sinned grievously" (1:8) with the inevitable result that "the Lord has become like an enemy, he has destroyed Israel" (Lam 2:5), there is, too, the serene assurance:

> For the Lord will not cast off forever
> but, though he cause grief, he will have compassion
> according to the abundance of his steadfast love;
> for he does not willingly afflict or grieve the sons of men
> (3: 31-33).

Even in these deeps of distress the heartening note of complaint still sounds:

> Why do you forget us forever,
> why do you so long forsake us?
> Restore us to yourself, O Lord, that we may be restored!
> renew our days as of old!
> Or have you utterly rejected us?
> Are you exceedingly angry with us? (5: 20-22).

"Have you utterly rejected us?" is not merely a rhetorical question; it carries overtones of exasperation worthy of Moses or Jeremiah. Here is a people bloody but unbowed—not in defiance of God but in robust confidence in his loving-kindness.

Another appendix to Jeremiah (in the Septuagint, the pre-Christian Greek version of the Old Testament) is Baruch—a writing much later than the age of Jeremiah's disciple-secretary. Its writer is very conscious of the glaring contrast between the holy God and his sinful people: "Righteousness belongs to the Lord our God, but confusion of face to us and our fathers, as at this day" (2:6; cf 1:15). The introduction to his prayer (1:15-2:10) is a candid confession of sin: "We have not entreated the favor of the Lord by turning away, each of us, from the thoughts of his wicked heart. . . We have not obeyed his voice, to walk in the statutes of the Lord which he set before us" (2: 8, 10). The prayer itself (2:11-3:8) recalls the great Exodus event. That is the basis of the exiles' confidence, not necessarily that they be restored to their homeland, but that, in exile, they may meet their God.

> O Lord Almighty, God of Israel, the soul in anguish and
> the weary spirit cry out to thee. Hear, O Lord, and have

mercy, for we have sinned before thee. . . Remember not
the iniquities of our fathers, but in this crisis remember thy
power and thy name. For you are the Lord our God, and
you, O Lord, will we praise. For you have put the fear of
you in our hearts in order that we should call upon your
name; and we will praise you in our exile, for we have put
away from our hearts all the iniquity of our fathers who
sinned before you (3: 1-2, 5-7).

EZRA and NEHEMIAH

The prayer of Ezra (Ez 9: 6-15) while it follows the
broad pattern we have observed, is specific in its import.
Ezra regards intermarriage with neighboring peoples as an
infringement of the law of Deuteronomy (Ez 9: 11-12; cf
Dt 7: 1-3) and as unfaithfulness to God—therefore, as sin.
He acknowledges the culpability of his people, and concludes:

> O Lord the God of Israel, thou art just, for we are left a
> remnant that has escaped, as at this day. Behold, we are
> before thee in our guilt, for none can stand before thee
> because of this (9:15).

A prayer of Nehemiah (Neh 1: 5-11), patently inspired by
Deuteronomy, nevertheless includes the characteristic
post-exilic confession of sin:

> O Lord God of heaven, the great and terrible God who
> keeps covenant and steadfast love with those who love him
> and keep his commandments; let thy ear be attentive, and
> thy eyes open, to hear the prayer of thy servant which I
> now pray before thee day and night for the people of Israel
> thy servants, confessing the sins of the people of Israel,
> which we have sinned against you. Yea, I and my father's
> house have sinned (Neh 1: 5-6).

A prayer of Ezra (Neh 9: 6-37) opens with the familiar
recall of the goodness and might of God shown in the
Exodus-event (9: 6-25). Then comes the "nevertheless"—

the inevitable infidelity: "Nevertheless they were disobedient and rebelled against you and cast your law behind their back and killed your prophets, who had warned them in order to turn them back to you. . ." (9: 26-31). Finally, there is the appeal to God: an appeal hidden and applied in the vivid presentation of distress:

> Now therefore, our God, the great and mighty and terrible God, who keep covenant and steadfast love, let not all the hardship seem little to you that has come upon us. . . You have been just in all that has come upon us, for you have dealt faithfully and we have acted wickedly. . . Behold, we are slaves this day; in the land that you gave to our fathers to enjoy its fruit and its good gifts, behold, we are slaves. . . and we are in great distress (Neh 9: 32-37).

It is enough to put the sorry case before the Lord. In his way and in his good time he will redeem the situation.

TOBIT and SIRACH

A prayer of Tobit (Tob 13: 1-8) takes its place among these others; it stresses more than they the benefit of repentance.

> He will afflict us for our iniquities;
> and again he will show mercy. . .
> If you turn to him with all your heart and with all your soul,
> to do what is true before him,
> then he will turn to you
> and will not hide his face from you.
> But see what he will do with you;
> give thanks to him with your full voice. . .
> Turn back, you sinners, and do right before him;
> who knows if he will accept you and have mercy on you?
>   (Tob 13: 5-6)

Sirach, too, contains a prayer that is at home here, though it was not explicit confession of sin but a prayer for

Israel (36: 1-17). It calls upon the mercy of the Lord and
asks the Lord to display his might before the nations.

> As in us you have been sanctified before them,
> so in them be you magnified before us;
> and let them know you, as we have known,
> that there is no God but you, O Lord (36: 4-5).

Hope of redemption rests on election and covenant: God
had freely chosen his people and had made it peculiarly his
own:

> Have mercy, O Lord, upon the people called by your
> name,
> upon Israel whom you have likened to a first-born son.
> Have pity on the city of your sanctuary,
> Jerusalem, the place of your rest (36: 12-13).

It is unthinkable that ever God should abandon his people.
This, too, will be the firm conviction of Paul: "I ask, then,
has God rejected his people? By no means!. . . God has
not rejected his people whom he foreknew!" (Rom 11:1-2).

ESTHER and JUDITH

In a moving prayer, Mordecai, guardian of the new Persian queen Esther, a Jewess, justifies his refusal to pay
deference to the powerful and vindictive Haman, enemy of
the Jews. He wants to make quite clear that his stance is
not motivated by arrogance.

> You know all things; you know, O Lord, that it was not in
> insolence or pride or for any love of glory that I did this
> and refused to bow down to this proud Haman. For I
> would have been willing to kiss the soles of his feet, to save
> Israel! But I did this, that I might not set the glory of man
> above the glory of God, and I will not bow down to any
> one but to you, who are my Lord; and I will not do these
> things in pride.

> And now, O Lord God and King, God of Abraham,
> spare your people. . . Hear my prayer, and have mercy
> upon your inheritance; turn our mourning into feasting,
> that we may live and sing praise to your name, O Lord; do
> not destroy the mouth of those who praise you (Esther 3:
> 12-17).

We have noted throughout the outspokenness of Moses,
Jeremiah and others. Yet, there is something especially touching
in this appeal of Mordecai. It does not have the brashness we
have seen before; it has a directness that is even more effective:
"Do not destroy the mouth of those who praise you"
(3: 17). The author of Esther stands in that forthright tradition.
He, too, can challenge his God—because he, too, knows his
God.

The most striking prayers in the Book of Judith are, not surprisingly, those of Judith herself—and will be seen in a later
chapter. The prayer of Uzziah (chief magistrate of the besieged
town of Bethulia) is noteworthy because it is fulsome in its praise
of the achievement of a woman. It is fair to observe that this
may be because Judith (the "Jewess") is an ideal representative
of Judaism. The prayer celebrates her daring slaying of
Holofernes—a victory won by her prayer (9: 2-14; 13: 4-5) and
her scrupulous observance of the law:

> O daughter, you are blessed by the Most High God above
> all women on earth; and blessed be the Lord God, who
> created the heavens and the earth, who has guided you to
> strike the head of the leader of our enemies. Your hope will
> never depart from the hearts of men, as they remember the
> power of God. May God grant this to be a perpetual honor
> to you, and may he visit you with blessings, because you
> did not spare your own life when our nation was brought
> low, but have avenged our ruin, walking in the straight
> path before our God (Judith 13: 18-20).

DANIEL

In the period shortly before the Maccabean revolt
(167-164 B.C.) we can place the origin of a Jewish party

called the *Hasidim* (the "Pious Ones"). Their characteristic attitude was loyalty to the Law at all costs and they vehemently opposed the spreading hellenistic influence on Jewish life. They wholeheartedly supported the Maccabean rising. The author of Daniel is plainly one of the Hasidim. He based his summons to courageous faith on the affirmation that God ruled the course of history. It is noteworthy that the prayers here, reflective of the Hasidim outlook, candidly admit the failures of Israel and appeal solely to the gracious goodness of Yahweh. Such is the prayer of Azariah (3: 26-45):

> You are just in all that you have done to us,
> for we have sinned and lawlessly departed from you,
> and have sinned in all things (3: 27-29).

Confession of sin is but a prelude to confident hope:

> Yet with a contrite heart and a humble spirit
> may we be accepted,
> as though it were with burnt offerings of rams and bulls,
> and with tens of thousands of fat lambs.
> Such may our sacrifice be in your sight this day,
> and may we wholly follow you,
> for there will be no shame for those who trust in you.
> And now with all our heart we follow you,
> we fear you and seek your face.
> Do not put us to shame,
> but deal with us in your forbearance
> and in your abundant mercy (3: 39-42).

A prayer of Daniel can fittingly round off this chapter. It is not only typical, it is the most moving of all these prayers of the chastened.

> O Lord, the great and terrible God, who keep covenant and steadfast love with those who love him and keep his commandments, we have sinned and done wrong and acted wickedly and rebelled, turning aside from your commandments and ordinances; we have not listened to your servants the prophets, who spoke in your name to our

kings, our princes, and our fathers, and to all the people of the land. To you, O Lord, belongs righteousness, but to us confusion of face, as at this day, to the men of Judah, to the inhabitants of Jerusalem, and to all Israel, those that are near and those that are far away, in all the lands to which you have driven them, because of the treachery which they have committed against you. To us, O Lord, belongs confusion of face, to our kings, to our princes, and to our fathers, because we have sinned against you. To the Lord our God belong mercy and forgiveness. . .

O Lord, according to all your righteous acts, let your anger and your wrath turn away from your city Jerusalem, your holy hill; because for our sins, and for the iniquities of our fathers, Jerusalem and your people have become a byword among all who are round about us. Now, therefore, O our God, hearken to the prayer of your servant and to his supplications, and for your own sake, O Lord, cause your face to shine upon your sanctuary, which is desolate. O my God, incline your ear and hear; open your eyes and behold our desolations, and the city which is called by your name; for we do not present our supplications before you on the ground of our righteousness, but on the ground of your great mercy.

O Lord, hear; O Lord forgive; O Lord, give heed and act; delay not, for your own sake, O my God, because your city and your people are called by your name (9: 4-9, 16-19).

The "great and terrible" God is the God who keeps steadfast love with his people. And to his people, beyond doubt, belongs "confusion of face." But the relationship of people and God is transformed when we hear: O Lord, hear— forgive—act—do not delay. Those who pray are those who have suffered the trauma of the Exile. They know that their God has responded far beyond their hope.

Six

Prayer of the Women

"I will make him a helper fit for him" (Genesis 2:18). The Yahwist-author of Genésis 2-3 has acknowledged the contemporary social status of woman in a Semitic culture: suffering in motherhood, chattel of her "lord" (3:16). But he has charmingly shown her as she was meant to be (2:21-24). The unhappy real woman of the Yahwist's experience was to be the typical Old Testament woman, but the picture was not wholly black. At all times and in all cultures there have been women who have risen above their lot. It would seem that this was notably so in Israel.

The women who figure in this chapter do so because of their prayer; they are not the only ones nor necessarily the greatest. Deborah and Judith are not more strong-willed than Rebekah (Gen 27: 5-17) and Bathsheba (1 Kgs 1: 11-31) and certainly not more so than the fanatical Jezebel (1 Kgs 19: 1-3; 21: 5-16) and the ruthless Athaliah (2 Kgs 11: 1-3). The touching child-yearning of Hannah is matched by the desire of other childless women. And the idyllic love-story of Tobit and Sarah is surpassed by the love-poetry of the Song of Songs. It is no anomaly that Israel is the Bride of Yahweh and Jerusalem is the Daughter of Zion. The Bible does not ignore womankind.

To us, twentieth-century citizens of the West, the place of women in the Bible seems subdued, very subdued. Their status is not calculated to bring joy to the heart of a feminist. But when we pause to think that the Old Testament is the product of a male-dominated culture, we should be impressed that women figure there to the extent that they do, and fill important roles. In the matter of prayer the men do not have it all their way. Women can and do pray too!

Rachel and Deborah

In the ongoing battle of wits between the uncle and the nephew, Laban and Jacob, the former won a round by foisting Leah as a wife on Jacob in place of Rachel —though Jacob ended by getting Rachel as well (Gen 29: 15-30). She was barren until "God remembered Rachel" (30: 22). He had "hearkened" to her (v 23): obviously she had prayed to him. And when her child Joseph was born she prayed, playing on his name, "May the Lord add to me another son!" (30: 24). Her prayer was answered, but at the price of her life; she died in giving birth to Benjamin (35: 16-18).

The "Song of Deborah" (Judges 5) is one of the oldest poems in the Bible. It celebrates a victory over the Canaanites in the early years of the settlement and praises or blames the tribes according as they had or had not joined the coalition led by Deborah and Barak. The song begins:

> Hear, O kings; give ear, O princes;
> to the Lord I will sing,
> I will make melody to the Lord, the God of Israel
> (Jg 5: 3).

and it closes:

> So perish all thine enemies, O Lord!
> But thy friends be like the sun as he rises in
> his might (5: 31).

Even though this song can scarcely be called a personal prayer, Deborah does rate a mention.

Hannah

The prayer of Hannah (1 Samuel 1: 9-18), even when one has listened to it or read it for the first time, may sound oddly familiar—that is because the Magnificat (Lk 1: 46-55) carries many echoes of it. The song itself is a late insertion into 1 Samuel. It sings of the care of the Lord for his faithful ones. He is no respecter of persons and his standards are not of the world.

The prayer strikes at once a note of confidence.

> My heart exults in the Lord; My strength is exalted in the Lord. . . There is none holy like the Lord, there is none beside thee; there is no rock like our God (1 Sam 2: 1-2).

Then Hannah proceeds to extol the paradoxical way of the Lord: the mighty are broken while the feeble find strength; those who abounded will beg for bread while the hungry will hunger no more (2: 4-5). It is surely because of the next contrast—"the barren has borne seven, but she who has many children is forlorn" (v 5)—that the song has found its present setting. That declaration is in place on the lips of one who, though barren, had, in answer to fervent prayer, become the mother of a son (1 Sam 1).

The former distress of Hannah, and her prayer, are movingly depicted. Hannah had come, with her husband Elkanah, to the shrine of Yahweh at Shiloh. "She was deeply distressed and prayed to the Lord, and wept bitterly" (1: 11). She vowed that if she were granted a son, he would be consecrated to the Lord. The priest Eli, who happened to see her in prayer, was upset by her demeanour: "As she continued praying before the Lord, Eli observed her mouth. Hannah was speaking in her heart; only her lips moved, and her voice was not heard; therefore Eli took her to be a drunken woman" (1: 12-13). This tells that it was normal for prayer to be spoken aloud. Hannah's prayer was so deep that it could find no words. She explains to Eli: "I am a woman sorely troubled. . . I have been pouring out my soul before the Lord" (1: 15). Eli was convinced not alone of her sincerity but that her prayer deserved to be heard: "Go in peace, and the Lord of Israel grant your petition which you have made to him" (1: 17). She became the mother of Samuel (1: 19-20).

To return to the song and its contrasts. The Lord is source of death and of life; he makes poor and rich, he humbles and exalts (2: 6-7). A clear reference to Job illustrates his freedom and his power:

> He raises up the poor from the dust; he lifts the needy from the ash heap, to make them sit with princes (2:8).

The wicked cannot win, for "not by might shall a man prevail" and the Lord "will guard the feet of his faithful ones" (2:9). Strangely, that is to say strangely in its present context of thanksgiving for motherhood, the song ends with a prayer for the king (2:10).

Sarah and Edna

We have met Sarah before—she who became the wife of young Tobias. But, previous to that happy event, she was an afflicted one, and her prayer voices her distress:

> Blessed art thou, O Lord my God, and blessed is thy holy and honoured name for ever. May all thy works praise thee for ever. And now, O Lord, I have turned my eyes and my face toward thee. Command that I be released from the earth and that I hear reproach no more. You know, O Lord, that I am innocent of any sin with man, or that I did not stain my name or the name of my father in the land of my captivity. I am my father's only child, and he has no child to be his heir, no near kinsmen or kinsman's son for whom I should keep myself as wife. Already seven husbands of mine are dead. Why should I live? But if it be

> not pleasing to you to take my life, command that respect
> be shown to me and pity be taken upon me, and that I hear
> reproach no more (Tobit 3: 11-15).

In prayer Sarah had found strength to resist the temptation
to take her life when life itself had become intolerable
(3:10). She was, of course, mistaken in imagining that
there was no near kinsman whom she might marry (v 15).
Soon one would be on the way to seek her hand, one who
would fall deeply in love with her at the mention of her
name (6: 9-17). The Lord had taken pity on her, and her
sorrow would turn to joy. Soon she would join with him in
prayer on their wedding night (8: 5-8).

There is the deep-felt womanly prayer of Edna as the
young couple set out to begin their new life together:
prayer of a mother for the welfare of her daughter, a
prayer of longing for grandchildren.

> The Lord of heaven bring you back safely, dear brother,
> and grant me to see your children by my daughter Sarah,
> that I may rejoice before the Lord. See, I am entrusting my
> daughter to you; do nothing to grieve her (10:12).

Esther

The story of Esther (second century B.C.) tells how a
beautiful young Jewess, guided by her wise uncle
Mordecai—she was an orphan—had become the queen of
the Persians (Esther 2: 1-17). Then, when at the instigation
of the wicked grand-vizier Haman, king Ahasuerus
(Xerxes) had proclaimed a pogrom of all Jews throughout
the Persian empire, Mordecai persuaded a reluctant Esther
that she must plead with the king for her people. He points
out that her unexpected station is providential: Who
knows whether you have not come to the kingdom for such
a time as this? (4: 14). Esther yields, but not before he has
agreed to her terms that all Jews in the Persian capital of
Susa will hold a solemn fast for three days.

Before taking the fateful step of approaching the king uninvited—for dramatic effect it is supposed that for anyone to approach the king without being summoned means death (4: 11)—Esther, "seized with deathly anxiety, fled to the Lord" (14: 1).
She prayed:

> O my Lord, you only are our King; help me who am alone and have no helper but you, for my danger is in my hand. Ever since I was born I have heard in the tribe of my family that you, O Lord, did take Israel out of all the nations, and our father from among all their ancestors, for an everlasting inheritance, and that you did do for them all that you did promise. And now we have sinned before you, and you have given us into the hands of our enemies, because we glorified their gods. You are righteous, O Lord! . . .
>
> O Lord, do not surrender your scepter to what has no being; and do not let them mock at our downfall. . .
>
> Remember, O Lord: make yourself known in this time of our affliction, and give me courage, O King of the gods and Master of all dominion! Put eloquent speech in my mouth before the lion. . .
>
> Save us by your hand, and help me, who am alone and have no helper but you, O Lord (14: 3-14).

So far, this is, obviously, a typical "prayer of the chastened." Esther goes on to protest that her royal station is not of her choosing. She has no joy in being queen; her only joy is in the Lord.

> You have knowledge of all things; and you know that I hate the splendor of the wicked and abhor the bed of the uncircumcised and of any alien. You know my necessity—that I abhor the sign of my proud position [her royal crown] which is upon my head on the days when I appear in public. I abhor it like a menstruous rag, and I do not wear it on the days when I am at leisure. And your servant has not eaten at Haman's table, and I have not honoured the king's feast or drunk the wine of the

libatious... Your servant has had no joy since the day that
I was brought here until now, except in You, O Lord God
of Abraham. O God, whose might is over all, hear the
voice of the despairing, and save me from the hands of
evildoers. And save me from my fear! (14: 15-19).

"And save me from my fear!" What a moving plea. Esther
is no heroine who boldly takes a drastic step, as Judith
will. She does what she knows is expected of her, but with
no great enthusiasm. Her only hope now is in the help of
her God. And her God did not fail her. What took place is
related with charm.

"On the third day, when she ended her prayer, she took
off the garments in which she had worshipped, and ar-
rayed herself in splendid attire. Then, majestically adorned,
after invoking the aid of the all-seeing God and Saviour,
she took her two maids with her, leaning daintily on one,
while the other followed carrying her train. She was ra-
diant with perfect beauty, and she looked happy, as if
beloved, but her heart was frozen with fear. When she had
gone through all the doors, she stood before the king. He
was seated on his royal throne, clothed in the full array of
his majesty, all covered with gold and precious stones. And
he was most terrifying.

"Lifting his face, flushed with splendor, he looked at her
in fierce anger. And the queen faltered, and turned pale
and faint, and collapsed upon the head of the maid who
went before her. Then God changed the spirit of the king
to gentleness, and in alarm he sprang from his throne and
took her in his arms until she came to herself. And he com-
forted her with soothing words, and said to her, 'What is
it, Esther? I am your brother. Take courage; you shall not
die, for our law applies only to the people. Come near.'

"Then he raised the golden scepter and touched it to her
neck; and he embraced her and said, 'Speak to me.' And
she said to him, 'I saw you, my lord, and your countenance
is full of grace.' But as she was speaking, she fell fainting.
And the king was agitated, and all his servants sought to
comfort her" (ch 15).

From now on, Esther is invincible. With her to speak for them, her people are no longer in danger. The all-powerful monarch, king of kings, is putty in the delicate hands of a Jewish maiden. It is wishful thinking, of course; yet it must have brought some comfort to the heart of a subject people. And, like Tobit, if on a more lavish scale, it is a story of answer to prayer.

Susanna

God's hearkening to the prayer of the innocent is a major theme of the tale of Susanna (Daniel 13). She had resisted, even under threat of disgrace and death, the lustful advances of two elders of the people (13: 5-23). Spitefully, they made good their threat; they accused Susanna of adultery and had her condemned to death. "Then Susanna cried out with a loud voice and said":

> O eternal God, who discern what is secret, who are aware of all things before they come to be, you know that these men have borne false witness against me. And now I am to die! Yet I have done none of the things that they have wickedly invented against me! (13: 42-43).

The Lord heard her cry. Through the instrumentality of the young Daniel he vindicated the innocence of Susanna and had the guilty condemned and punished (13: 45-61). The prayer of the virtuous is mighty before the Lord.

Judith

In the story of Judith—the name means "the Jewess"— a downtrodden people gave expression, around the turn of the first century B.C., to its dream of deliverance. Again, as with Esther, it is remarkable that the deliverer is a woman.. Perhaps the intention is that this deliverance would stand out more starkly as an achievement of God.

Whether or not this is so, it must be that by such a story the honour of womankind is enhanced.

The Jewish nation is again in deadly danger. Holofernes, with his mighty Assyrian army, is besieging the town of Bethulia (Judith 7: 1-3) which, for the purpose of the story, guarded the only way of access to Jerusalem. If Bethulia falls, the land is doomed. The terrified defenders want to surrender, but the governor, Uzziah, prevails on them to hold out for five days. If God has not acted by then, he will capitulate (7: 23-31).

Judith, a beautiful and virtuous widow, is appalled by such lack of confidence in God. She boldly upbraids the rulers of her people—and reads them a lesson in theology.

"Listen to me, rulers of the people of Bethulia! What you have said to the people today is not right; you have even sworn and pronounced this oath between God and you, promising to surrender the city to our enemies unless the Lord turns and helps us within so many days. Who are you, that you have put God to the test this day, and are setting yourselves up in the place of God among the sons of men? You are putting the Lord Almighty to the test—but you will never know anything! You cannot plumb the depths of the human heart, nor find out what a man is thinking; how do you expect to search out God, who made all these things, and find out his mind or comprehend his thought? No, my brethren, do not provoke the Lord our God to anger. For if he does not choose to help us within these five days, he has power to protect us within any time he pleases, or even to destroy us in the presence of our enemies. Do not try to bind the purposes of the Lord our God; for God is not like man, to be threatened, nor like a human being, to be won over by pleading. Therefore, while we wait for his deliverance, let us call upon him to help us, and he will hear our voice, if it pleases him...Now therefore, brethren, let us set an example to our brethren [in Judea] for their lives depend upon us, and the sanctuary and the temple and the altar rest upon us. In spite of everything let us give thanks to the Lord our God, who is putting us to the test as he did our forefathers...For he has not tried us with fire, as he did them, to search their hearts, nor has he taken revenge upon us, but the Lord scourges those who draw near to him, in order to admonish them" (8: 11-17, 24-25, 27).

Shamefacedly, Uzziah agrees that Judith is right. There is, however, the problem that the besieged town is almost out of water! (8: 28-30). "So pray for us, since you are a devout woman, and the Lord will send us rain to fill our cisterns and we will no longer be faint" (v 31). Judith is made of sterner metal than Esther and has already determined on a bold stroke. "Listen to me. I am about to do a thing which will go down through all generations of our descendants...Only, do not try to find out what I plan; for I will not tell you until I have finished what I am about to do" (8: 32, 34). A resolute woman indeed!

Judith was bold because her strength was in the Lord. "Then Judith fell upon her face, and put ashes on her head, and uncovered the sackcloth she was wearing; and at the very time when the evening's incense was being offered in the house of God in Jerusalem, Judith cried out to the Lord with a loud voice" (9: 1). She begins: "Give to me, a widow, the strength to do what I plan. By the deceit of my lips strike down the slave with the prince and the prince with his servant; crush their arrogance by the hand of a woman" (9: 9-10). And she concludes with impassioned words:

> For your power depends not upon numbers, nor your
> might upon men of strength; for you are
> God of the lowly,
> helper of the oppressed,
> upholder of the weak,
> protector of the forlorn,
> saviour of those without hope.
> Hear, O hear me, God of my faith, God of the
> inheritance of Israel, Lord of heaven and earth,
> Creator of the waters, King of all your creation,
> hear my prayer! Make my deceitful words to be
> their wound and stripe, for they have planned
> cruel things against your covenant, and against

> your consecrated house, and against the top of Zion,
> and against the house possessed by your children.
> And cause your whole nation and every tribe to know and
> understand that you are God, the God of all power
> and might, and that there is no other who
> protects the people of Israel but you alone! (9: 11-14)

Perhaps nowhere else is the faithful Israelite's sense of total dependence on God so forcefully expressed.

Therefore, Judith began to put her plan into effect. First she adorned herself "and made herself very beautiful, to entice the eyes of all men who might see her" (10: 4). As one who had always scrupulously observed the Law, she takes care to pack an adequate supply of "kosher" food (10: 5). Accompanied by a maid, Judith set out toward the enemy lines; they were promptly arrested by an Assyrian patrol. She passed herself off as a deserter from the doomed town, one prepared to betray a secret way into the heart of the country. Bemused by her beauty, the troops took her to their general; and her arrival in the camp caused quite a stir! (10: 17-19). Holofernes, too, was captivated and accepted her story without question (ch 11).

Judith cleverly arranged that she and her maid could leave the camp at night, as they did three nights in a row, so preparing her escape route (ch 12). On the fateful fourth night Holofernes held a banquet and invited Judith, planning to have his way with her afterwards. He was so happy at her presence that "he drank a great quantity of wine, much more than he had ever drunk in any one day since he was born" (14: 20). When Judith did, at last, find herself alone with Holofernes he was "stretched out on his bed, for he was overcome with wine" (13: 2). She was safe—and now was her chance to carry out her resolve. She prayed:

> O Lord God of all might, look in this hour upon the work
> of my hands for the salvation of Jerusalem. For now is the
> time to help your inheritance, and to carry out my under-
> taking for the destruction of the enemies who have risen up
> against us (13: 4-5).

Judith laid hold of Holofernes' sword and with the cry, "Give me strength this day, O Lord God of Israel!" (v 7), struck off his head. With the severed head hidden in their food bag, she and her maid passed through the Assyrian outposts and came to Bethulia where they displayed undeniable proofs of a mission accomplished (13: 15). The author is careful to insist that more than Judith's life was guarded and has her declare: "As the Lord has protected me in the way I went, it was my face that tricked him into his destruction, and yet he committed no act of sin with me, to defile and shame me" (13: 16).

Uzziah is fulsome in his praise of the valiant Judith and blesses the God who had inspired her: "Oh daughter, you are blessed by the Most High above all women on earth; and blessed by the Lord God, who created the heavens and the earth, who has guided you to strike the head of the leader of our enemies. Your hope will never depart from the hearts of men, as they remember the power of God. May God grant this to be a perpetual honor to you, and may he visit you with blessings, because you did not spare your own life when our nation was brought low, but have avenged our ruin, walking in the straight path before our God" (13: 18-20).

With their general dead, the Assyrians panicked and were routed (chs 14-15). Judith became the toast of the nation. Joakim, the high priest, and "the senate of the people of Israel" came from Jerusalem to greet her and sing her praises: "You are the exaltation of Jerusalem, you are the great glory of Israel, you are the great pride of our nation! You have done all this single-handed; you have done great good to Israel, and God is well pleased with it. May the Almighty Lord bless you for ever!" And all the people said, "So be it" (15: 9-10).

The long canticle of Judith rounds off the dramatic story. For the greater part, it is a poetic version of her exploit, but it runs on into a hymn of beauty.

> O Lord, you are great and glorious,
> wonderful in strength, invincible.

Let all your creatures serve you,
for you spoke, and they were made.
You sent forth your spirit, and it formed them;
there is none that can resist your voice.
For the mountains shall be shaken to their
foundations with the waters;
at your presence the rocks shall melt like wax,
but to those who fear you
you will continue to show mercy.
For every sacrifice as a fragrant offering is a
small thing,
and all fat for burnt offerings to you
is a very little thing,
but he who fears the Lord shall be great
for ever (16: 13-16).

"Fear of the Lord" is commitment to him, it is trustful service. This God of power and might holds no terror for his
faithful ones. True greatness lies in serving him alone. It
may be that it needs a woman to tell what faithfulness
means.

Seven

The Book of Prayer

The Chronicler, we have noted, had discerned the role of David in the development of the cult and liturgy of Israel. He had made Jerusalem the religious center of the nation; he had planned to build a temple. His reputation as a religious poet was firm. It is not surprising, then, that the book of psalms has been attributed to him. He stood at the beginning of a process that culminated in the psalter.

In reality, the psalter is the hymn-book of the Second Temple (that was built after the return from Babylonian Exile, 587-536). Most of the psalms are later than David's time. These one hundred and fifty poems are varied: psalms of praise, of petition, of thanksgiving...They vary, too, in poetic quality and religious depth. But all are inspired by faith in the God of Israel and find their place in his worship. And, as nineteen centuries of Christianity have shown, they fit smoothly into the liturgical life of the Christian Church.

While the Psalter ended by being Israel's book of liturgical prayer (and the liturgy is not our concern here) it is self-evident that not a few of the psalms began life as individual prayers. We will glance at some that seem to have been surely such. Besides, it would be an anomaly to write of prayer in the Bible and leave the psalter wholly aside.

Complaint

The prayer of the faithful Israelite seems sooner or later—sooner rather than later—to voice the complaint: "How long, O Lord, how long?" It is a refreshing characteristic because it is so honest. We all do feel that the Lord, as often as not, is deaf to our appeal. The psalmists undoubtedly felt so.

> How long, O Lord? Will you forget me for ever?
> How long will you hide your face from me?
> How long must I bear pain in my soul,
> and have sorrow in my heart all the day? (Ps 13:1-2)

Most notable is that complaint so famous in Christian tradition: Jesus, Jew of Jews, had cried out to his Father (cf Mk 15: 34).

> My God, my God, why have you forsaken me?
> Why are you so far from helping me, from
> the words of my groaning?
> Oh my God, I cry by day, but you do not answer;
> and by night, but find no rest (Ps 22: 1-2).

Always, of course, there is the accompanying trust.

> But I have trusted in your steadfast love;
> my heart shall rejoice in your salvation (13: 5)

> Yet you are he who took me from the womb;
> who did keep me safe upon my mother's breasts.
> Upon you was I cast from my birth,
> and since my mother bore me you have been my God.
> Be not far from me,
> for trouble is near and there is none to help (22: 9-11).

> In you, O Lord, do I seek refuge;
> let me never be put to shame;
> in your righteousness deliver me!
> Incline your ear to me, rescue me speedily!

> Be you a rock of refuge for me,
> a strong fortress to save me!...
> Into your hand I commit my spirit;
> you have redeemed me, O Lord, faithful God (31: 1-5).

Petition

The psalmist, in distress, pleads his cause, unabashed, before God—and nothing is lost in the telling.

> I am weary with my moaning;
> every night I flood my bed with tears;
> I drench my couch with my weeping (6: 6).

> I am poured out like water,
> and all my bones are out of joint...
> my strength is dried up like a potsherd,
> and my tongue cleaves to my jaws;
> you lay me in the dust of death (22: 14-15).

> I am the scorn of all my adversaries,
> a horror to my neighbors,
> an object of dread to my acquaintances;
> those who see me in the street flee from me (31: 11).

A keen awareness of a personal God, a merciful and understanding God, pervades these prayers:

> When I am afraid, I put my trust in you.
> In God, whose word I praise,
> in God I trust without a fear.
> What can flesh do to me? (56: 3-4)

And as for distress—no sigh, no tear goes astray:

> You have kept count of my tossings;
> put my tears in your bottle!
> Are they not in your book? (56: 8).

All because God is like that!

> For his anger is but for a moment,
> and his favor is for a lifetime.
> Weeping may tarry for the night,
> but joy comes with the morning (30: 5).

There are the two well-known psalms, no less beautiful for being so familiar. The *De Profundis* (Out of the Depths):

> I wait for the Lord, my soul waits,
> and in his word I hope;
> my soul waits for the Lord
> more than watchmen for the morning (130: 5-6).

And the *Miserere* (Have Mercy) the classic prayer of repentance:

> Have mercy on me, O God,
> according to your steadfast love;
> according to your abundant mercy, blot out
> my transgressions...
> Hide your face from my sins,
> and blot out all my iniquities.
> Create in me a clean heart, O God,
> and put a new and right spirit within me...
> The sacrifice acceptable to God is a broken spirit;
> a broken and contrite heart, O God, you will not
> despise (51: 1, 9-10, 17).

Always that admirable dignity. The sinner has no need to grovel before this God. He is a God who always respects his servants, even when they fail him. He is a God who welcomes their honest acknowledgment of failure. He is a God who reinstates them without question.

Thanksgiving

Biblical man was grateful. If, in distress, he prayed earnestly to the Lord, he then thanked the Lord with a generous heart when he had been helped and delivered. He understood that thanksgiving is praise of the Lord. And he knew how to express his gratitude with graciousness.

> I love the Lord, because he has heard
> my voice and my supplications.
> Because he inclined his ear to me,
> therefore I will call on him as long as I live...
> Gracious is the Lord, and righteous;
> our God is merciful.
> The Lord preserves the simple;
> when I was brought low, he saved me.
> Return, O my soul, to your rest;
> for the Lord has dealt bountifully with you
>   (116: 1-2, 5-7).

> On the day I called, you did answer me,
> my strength of soul you did increase...
> The Lord will fulfill his purpose for me;
> your steadfast love, O Lord, endures for ever.
> Do not forsake the work of your hands (138: 3, 8).

My God and My All!

A remarkable feature of the psalms is that the psalmist can assert that God is his all. His earnestness leaves no room for doubt. We must believe that he had, indeed, found the meaning of life.

> For God alone my soul waits in silence,
> for my hope is from him.
> He only is my rock and my salvation,
> my fortress; I shall not be shaken.
> On God rests my deliverance and my honour;
> my mighty rock, my refuge is God (62: 5-7).

God is not a distant God. Though enthroned in the heavens he is near and accessible to his servants.

> To you I lift up my eyes,
> O You who are enthroned in the heavens!
> Behold, as the eyes of servants

> look to the hand of their master,
> or the eyes of a maid to the hand of her mistress,
> so our eyes look to the Lord our God,
> till he have mercy upon us (123: 1-2).

And mercy is what they find:

> He does not deal with us according to our sins,
> nor requite us according to our iniquities.
> For as the heavens are high above the earth,
> so great is his steadfast love toward those
> who fear him;
> as far as the east is from the west,
> so does he remove our transgressions from us.
> As a father pities his children,
> so the Lord pities those who fear him (103: 10-13).

It follows that God is joy and hope and rest.

> My soul is feasted as with marrow and fat,
> and my mouth praises you with joyful lips,
> when I think of you upon my bed,
> and meditate on you in the watches of the night;
> for you have been my help,
> and in the shadow of your wings I sing for joy.
> My soul clings to you;
> your right hand upholds me (63: 5-8).

God brings the peace that the world cannot give.

> I have calmed and quieted my soul,
> like a child quieted at its mother's breast;
> like a child that is quieted is my soul (131: 2).

Praise

A God who so fills one's life is surely worthy of praise.
The psalmists do not stint.

> Blessed be the name of the Lord
> from this time forth and for evermore!

> From the rising of the sun to its setting
> the name of the Lord is to be praised! (113: 2-3)

> Praise the Lord, O my soul!
> I will praise the Lord as long as I live;
> I will sing praises to my God while I have being (146: 1-2).

God is Creator, and his creation proclaims his glory. Yet it needs man—to whom he has granted dominion over all his works (Ps 8)—to give fuller voice to the hymn of nature.

> O God, how manifold are your works!
> In wisdom you have made them all;
> the earth is full of your creatures.
> Yonder is the sea, great and wide,
> which teems with things innumerable,
> living things both small and great.
> There go the ships,
> and Leviathan which you did form to sport in it
>   (104: 24-26).

The priestly author of the creation-story (Genesis 1) could declare: "And God saw everything that he had made, and behold, it was very good" (Genesis 1: 31). Everything that exists has purpose—even the legendary sea-monsters. They sport in the mighty water, to the amusement of their Maker!

Praise of the Lord is a school of wisdom:

> Great are the works of the Lord,
> studied by all who have pleasure in them...
> The fear of the Lord is the beginning of wisdom;
> a good understanding have all who practice it.
> His praise endures for ever! (Ps 111: 2, 10)

The wise man is one who seeks the Lord and finds him. And the way of seeking and of finding is the way of prayer.

II. The New Testament

Introduction

The Israelite was a man of prayer—the evidence is impressive, is compelling. It is to be expected that among the new people of God prayer will have a central place. Jesus himself prayed to the Father, prayed out of his dependence and his need. Jesus taught us to pray, taught us to turn, in trust, to an Abba. Jesus prayed, and there is example. We pray, and there is response.

Prayer is a Christian need, and Paul has shown that prayer can inspire and sustain. The Christian way is a path, a path best walked by the childlike one who skips ahead of Father and Son. We feel that we dare not take him at his word for that would be foolishness. Yet, he has said: "Unless you become as little children..." Is the demand as crazy as it seems? Would not this be a wondrous world if it were run by children, by *real* children, the bright-eyed, the innocent, the questing, for theirs is the kingdom of heaven! That is what Jesus said.

Paradoxically, Jesus uttered his invitation in the shadow of the cross. We are children of God and should turn, with childlike directness, to our Father. But, in this world, we are sisters and brothers of the Brother who walked his way to Calvary. The Christian way, lived by Jesus, so firmly proposed by him and by his earliest disciples, is a way that challenges us. It is a way we dare not walk alone. But we are not alone, for he is with us.

We meet him in our prayer and keep step with him on the way. He has taught us to pray to the Father...and we have learned to pray to him. Paul, faithful disciple, has shown us how we ought to pray—and his disciples have learned well at his school. There are others who can and do guide us. There are the "poor" who put their whole trust in God and live lives of faith. One attuned to the Spirit can bring to us echoes of the prayer of heaven. In many and varied ways we are taught to pray. But the wellspring of Christian prayer will ever be the Son, and its inspiration the Spirit of the Son.

Eight

Prayer of Jesus

"Descended from David according to the flesh" (Rom 1: 3), Jesus was a son of Israel. As a committed son of Israel he was by definition a man of prayer. Apart from Luke, who had a special interest in prayer, the evangelists do not tend to elaborate on Jesus' prayer-life. That is not surprising. Simply, they, like him, took prayer for granted. We, Christians of another culture and of the twentieth century, cannot afford to be so casual. We demand reasons for everything, and we do ask why we should pray in the first place. The realization that Jesus was a man of prayer may give us pause.

Jesus prayed because prayer is a factor of our human condition. His father was the Creator, the Sustainer of all. As man, Jesus was wholly dependent on this God. He turned, spontaneously, to a Father who would support him, who would back him in his endeavours. True, he was one sent, one who had to plough his own furrow. But he was not alone, because the Father was with him.

The prayer of Jesus, by example and not by contrived design, is meant to alert the disciple to his or her dependence on God. If the Son found a need and a joy in converse with his Father he could expect that the other children of God, his brothers and sisters, would, too, experience that want and that happiness.

The astounding fact is that Jesus, as our high priest, has not ended his prayer. Returned to the Father he has no need, anymore, to pray for himself. Henceforth he is the high priest who prays *for us*, who makes intercession for us, without respite (cf Heb 7: 25).

It ought not surprise us that the prayer of Jesus should figure in the gospel of Luke. The third evangelist shows a notable interest in prayer, he could not have overlooked the prayer of the Lord. It is he who tells us that Jesus prayed at the Baptism: "Now when all the people were baptized, and when Jesus also had been baptized and was praying, the heaven was opened, and the Holy Spirit descended upon him in bodily form as a dove, and a voice came from heaven, 'Thou art my beloved Son; with thee I am well pleased'" (Lk 3: 21-22). Luke indeed gives the impression that it was in response to the prayer of Jesus that the Holy Spirit came upon him. And not impression only; it is Luke's intent that we should see it so. Later (11: 13) we learn that the heavenly Father gives the Holy Spirit to those who ask. And Jesus' prayer was a plea to the Father—not unlike the prayer of Job, though here apart from the context of distress—that God would manifest himself, would declare their relationship.

Jesus in Prayer

A phrase of Luke is revealing when we compare parallel gospel passages. Mark and Matthew both agree that Jesus, on coming to "his own country" (which Luke names as Nazareth) on a sabbath, began to teach (Mk 6: 2; Mt 13: 54). Luke effectively makes his own point: Jesus "went to the synagogue, as his custom was, on the sabbath day" (Lk 4: 16)—Jesus is characterized as a "regular church-goer."

Luke does not have it all his own way. One might even say that, because of Luke's avowed interest in prayer, reference to the prayer of Jesus by the other evangelists could have added weight. At least it assures us that Luke had latched on to a firm datum of the tradition. There can be no doubt at all that Jesus did pray. For that matter, even if the gospels had no word of his prayer, we could still be certain that he did pray. What we have seen of the Old Testament assures us that every sincere son of Israel was a man of prayer. But we do not need to speculate; the evidence is compelling. Mark, with his attractive candor, tells us that Jesus' addiction to prayer was something of a trial to his disciples. The evangelist has given a sample day in the early Galilean ministry, at Capernaum (Mk 1: 21-34), a day of enthusiasm and of great promise. His disciples, caught up in the enthusiasm, were chagrined when Jesus was missing (v 37).

> And in the morning, a great while before day, he rose and went out to a lonely place, and there he prayed (1: 35).

Typically, Mark has said so much in so few words. Jesus had slept ("he rose"), had snatched a few hours of sleep. For his mission he needed deeper refreshment, a more potent source of energy, and he found it in prayer to the Father.

Back to Luke again and to another key moment of the ministry: the call of the Twelve. For all three synoptists this is a significant turn. Yet, as at the Baptism, only Luke connects it with prayer of Jesus. He thereby endows the moment with a special solemnity.

> In these days he went out into the hills to pray; and all night he continued in prayer to God (Lk 6: 12).

If it were not for Mk 1: 35 we might assume that this night-vigil of Jesus was only in view of this decisive moment. The combined evidence would suggest that night prayer was a regular practice of his.

All three synoptists point to three key-points of the ministry: baptism, call of the Twelve, and transfiguration. Consistently, Luke, and he alone, speaks of prayer of Jesus at the third episode too.

> Now about eight days after these sayings he took with him
> Peter and John and James, and went up on the mountain
> to pray. And as he was praying, the appearance of his
> countenance was altered...(Lk 9: 28-29; cf Mk 9: 2;
> Mt 17: 1).

The transfiguration-scene is, by any standard, mysterious. Luke may have given us the clue as to the source of it: in prayer to the Father, Jesus was rapt in ecstasy, to the wonder of his disciples. Probably in the tradition, certainly by the evangelists, the incident was built up into its now familiar proportion.

At the multiplication of loaves John joins the others in reference to a prayer of Jesus: he "blessed" or "gave thanks"—a typically Jewish designation of prayer (Mk 6: 41; 8: 6; Mt 14: 19; 15: 35; Lk 9: 16; Jn 6: 11). Mark specifies that "he looked up to heaven." In all four gospels the feeding miracle carries manifest eucharistic overtones. In fact, the "blessing" or "giving thanks" is eucharistic language, reflecting the language of the Last Supper narratives: Mk 14: 22-23; Mt 26: 26-27; Lk 22: 17,19.

Prayers of Jesus

Mention of Jesus at prayer is relatively frequent in the gospels but only rarely, in the synoptics, are we given any words of prayer. Matthew and Luke, however, have preserved a lovely prayer of his. Characteristically, their introductions to it differ: "At that time Jesus declared" (Mt); "In that same hour he rejoiced in the Holy Spirit and said" (Lk):

> I thank thee, Father, Lord of heaven and earth, that thou
> hast hidden these things from the wise and understanding
> and revealed them to babes; yea, Father, for such was thy
> gracious will (Mt 11: 25-26; Lk 10: 21).

It is a prayer which brings consolation to all the "little ones" who feel that they have done nothing more than believe. If they have indeed listened they have already done a "good work." Their achievement may seem, in their eyes, a little thing. Because it is a gift of the Father it is of priceless worth. Both evangelists then go on, in strangely Johannine terms, to stress the unique relationship of Father and Son, and to explain why Jesus had joyfully thanked the Father for his gracious gift to the little ones:

> All things have been delivered to me by my Father; and no one knows who the Son is except the Father, or who the Father is except the Son and any one to whom the Son chooses to reveal him (Mt 11: 27; Lk 10: 22).

And Matthew adds the heartening invitation which, we shall see, is an incitement to trustful prayer (Mt 11: 28-30).

Jesus prayed not only for himself—again we are beholden to Luke. He has told us how it was that Peter was able to rise again after his dismal failure. In warning him that he would deny his Master, Jesus had assured him of his own efficacious prayer on his behalf:

> Simon, Simon, behold, Satan has demanded to have you, that he might sift you like wheat, but I have prayed for you that your faith may not fail; and when you have turned again, strengthen your brethren. (Lk 22: 31-32)

These words of Jesus sound not only for Simon but for every Christian who, at one time or other, has denied his Lord. He is ever the one interceding on our behalf (cf Heb 7: 25).

A more poignant prayer of Jesus was on the cross:

> Father forgive them; for they do not know what they do (Lk 23: 34).

It is a prayer that, happily, has echoed throughout Christian history—a prayer which inspired the prayer of the dying Stephen: "Lord, do not hold this sin against them" (Acts 7: 60). That prayer of Jesus, prayed in their turn by countless nameless disciples, far outweighs the

paeans of triumphalism. Jesus had firmly, sternly even, in-
culcated the demand of forgiveness. When it came to it, he
practiced what he preached. He who had bidden his
disciples: "Love your enemies" knows how to pray for
those who brought about his death. There can be no Christian prayer more pleasing to the Father.

Gethsemane

If Jesus could pray for others it was because he knew,
from experience, what it was to know distress and to pray
out of the heart of it. In some ways the painful
Gethsemane episode is the most comforting in the gospels.
There we see Jesus at his most human. Up to now he had
gone resolutely to meet his fate. Luke would suggest a certain eagerness: "When the days drew near for him to be
received up, he set his face to go to Jerusalem" (Lk 9: 51).
But now, when the dread moment is upon him, "he began
to be greatly distressed and troubled" (Mk 14: 33)—it is
almost impossible to convey adequately the force of
Mark's Greek: Jesus is shattered.

It had become clearer and clearer to Jesus what it was
that the Father seemed to be asking of him. He needed to
be assured that what God seemed to ask he really did ask.

> Abba, Father, all things are possible to thee; remove this
> cup from me; yet not what I will but what thou wilt (Mk
> 14: 36).

This is the first time, in Mark's gospel, that Jesus ad-
dresses his Father as Abba—the familiar title seems to be
wrenched from him at this awful moment. He prays, explicitly, that the cup may be taken from him, if such be
God's will. He does not contemplate suffering and a horri-
ble death with stoic calm. He is appalled at the prospect; he
knows fear. He is brave as he rises above his dread to embrace what it is God asks. But he must know if the path
that opens before him is indeed the way that God would
have him walk. He finds assurance in prayer: "And again

he went away and prayed, saying the same words"
(14: 39); "And being in an agony he prayed more earnestly" (Lk 22: 44). His prayer did not go unanswered; as the
letter to the Hebrews puts it: "he was heard for his godly
fear" (Heb 5: 7). In traditional biblical imagery, Luke has
concretized the heavenly response: "And there appeared
to him an angel from heaven, strengthening him" (Lk
22: 43). We are reminded of Tobit and Sarah and the
angelic answer to their prayer.

Earlier we had described the books of Tobit and of
Judith as being, in some measure, treatises on prayer. They
necessarily fade before this harrowing yet comforting
passage. Gethsemane did stir the Christian conscience. The
episode figures not only in the synoptics, (Mk 14: 32-42;
Mt 26: 36-46; Lk 22: 40-46) but in Hebrews—"In the days
of his flesh, Jesus offered up prayers and supplications,
with loud cries and tears, to him who was able to save him
from death, and he was heard for his godly fear" (Heb
5: 7)—and in John:

> Now is my soul troubled. And what shall I say, "Father
> save me from this hour?" No, for this purpose I have come
> to this hour. Father, glorify thy name (Jn 12: 27-28).

The Jesus who prays is recognizably the Johannine Jesus,
but the moment is doubtlessly that of Gethsemane.

Gethsemane is a lesson in prayer. It points out to the
disciples of Jesus the way of coping with their own
Gethsemanes. "Does God really ask this of me?" It is a
question that finds its answer in prayer. There will be no
angel to comfort us. There will be something more
precious: the comfort, felt deep within, of God's
assurance. What he asks of us must still be faced, as Jesus
went to suffering and death. But it will be faced with calm.
So it is no longer a shattered Jesus who rises from prayer
but one who boldly summons his disciples: "Rise, let us be
going" (Mk 14: 42). And it is, too, a fruit of the prayer of
Gethsemane that Luke can fittingly phrase the last words
of Jesus: "Father, into thy hands I commit my spirit" (Lk

23: 46). Because he had wholly accepted what the Father willed, his death was a prayer.

The Father

In the fourth gospel, as we shall see, Jesus speaks of prayer, of the disciples' prayer to him, or in his name to the Father. But this evangelist also shows Jesus himself in prayer to the Father—on at least three occasions. Jesus had come to the tomb of Lazarus. Before he will summon the dead man back to life, he turns to the Father:

> And Jesus lifted up his eyes and said, "Father, I thank thee that thou hast heard me. I know that thou hearest me always, but I have said this on account of the people standing by, that they may believe that thou didst send me" (11: 41-42).

Because Jesus is one with the Father (10: 30), because his whole concern is to do the will of the Father (4: 34), he can declare with absolute confidence that the Father hears him at this moment because he hears him at every moment. He rejoices that the bystanders will, through him, see the power of the Father. He rejoices that the great deed of restoring life will move them to recognize in Jesus the one sent by the Father, and thus they will come to know the Father and find life in their turn. For this raising of Lazarus is a "sign"—the promise that Jesus will give eternal life to those who will receive it.

The prayer of Jesus in 12: 27-28—"Now is my soul troubled. And what shall I say, 'Father save me from this hour?' No, for this purpose I have come to this hour. Father, glorify thy name"—is a variant of the synoptic Gethsemane prayer. Yet it has a typically Johannine cast. Jesus prays not that he may be spared but that he be sustained through this "hour." For John the hour of death-and-resurrection is supremely the hour of Jesus' revelation of the Father—the "glorification" of the Father. We meet the Jesus who has passed through the trial of Gethsemane

and is calmly set on accomplishing his given task
(cf 19: 30).

The most solemn prayer of Jesus, and not only in John,
but the most solemn prayer as such, is the great prayer of
John 17—the priestly and royal prayer. This prayer is, in
its way, a commentary on the passion of Jesus which
reflects the drift of the fourth gospel's emphasis: the coming of Jesus, revealer of the Father, into this world
(17: 1-12), then the return of Jesus to the Father
(17: 13-20). Structurally, though, the prayer falls into three
parts, as Jesus prays for himself (1-5), for his disciples
(6-19), and for the community of the future who will
"believe through their word" (20-26).

Prayer to the Father

> When Jesus had spoken these words, he lifted up his eyes
> to heaven and said, "Father, the hour has come; glorify thy
> Son that the Son may glorify thee, since thou hast given
> him power over all flesh, to give eternal life to all whom
> thou hast given him. And this is eternal life, that they
> know thee the only true God, and Jesus Christ whom thou
> hast sent. I glorified thee on earth, having accomplished
> the work which thou gavest me to do; and now, Father,
> glorify thou me in thy own presence with the glory which I
> had with thee before the world was made" (Jn 17: 1-5).

Now is the "hour," the hour of death-and-resurrection.
It is the glory of Jesus—"glory" being the revelation of
God in power. Only in death-and-resurrection does Jesus
fully reveal himself, and reveal the Father. And only by
laying down his own life for his friends, out of love, is
Jesus able to give the life-giving Spirit (cf 7: 39). "Glorify
thy Son": the "glorifying" of the Son necessarily involves
the glorifying of the Father because the self-disclosure of
Jesus is geared to the revelation of the unseen God.

If the Son has been given power over "all flesh"—all
mankind—it is that he may bestow "eternal life." Eternal
life is "knowledge": to leave oneself free to receive eternal

life one must know, one must have experienced, the loving relationship of Father and Son. True, Jesus' whole concern had been to make the Father known. Yet, the "hour" of his death and resurrection is the supreme moment of that revelation. And so Jesus prays to the Father.

Prayer for the Disciples

> I have manifested thy name to the men whom thou gavest me out of the world; thine they were, and thou gavest them to me, and they have kept thy word. Now they know that everything thou hast given me is from thee; for I have given them the words which thou gavest me, and they have received them and know in truth that I came from thee; and they have believed that thou didst send me. I am praying for them; I am not praying for the world but for those whom thou hast given me, for they are thine; all mine are thine, and thine are mine, and I am glorified in them. And now I am no more in the world, but they are in the world, and I am coming to thee. Holy Father, keep them in thy name which thou hast given me, that they may be one, even as we are one. While I was with them, I kept them in thy name which thou hast given me; I have guarded them, and none of them is lost but the son of perdition, that the scripture might be fulfilled. But now I am coming to thee; and these things I speak in the world, that they may have my joy fulfilled in themselves. I have given them thy word; and the world has hated them because they are not of the world, even as I am not of the world. I do not pray that thou shouldst take them out of the world, but that thou shouldst keep them from the evil one. They are not of the world, even as I am not of the world. Sanctify them in the truth; thy word is truth. As thou didst send me into the world, so I have sent them into the world. And for their sake I consecrate myself, that they also may be consecrated in truth (17: 6-19).

Jesus prays for his disciples present at the meal (ch 13)—he had taken care to make his Father known to them.

Indeed, they were the Father's gift to him in the first place—they know that the Father is the source of all that Jesus has done for them. Jesus has given them "the words" of the Father—he has revealed the Father. Now he is the high priest.

Jesus had come into the world because God so loved the world that he gave his only Son (3: 16), in order to save that world of men (v 17). But the world would not face the light; the saving gift had been turned into judgment (vv 18-19). Jesus, who is now sending his disciples into the world to speak again his word of salvation, cannot pray for that hostile world. The disciples are being sent, as Jesus was sent, to challenge the world, so that men might, at last, turn from darkness to light. He prays for those whom he leaves behind to carry on his work. He commits them to the Father's care and prays especially that they may know among themselves the warm communion of Father and Son. He reminds the Father that he, on earth, had kept and guarded them.

Verse 13 opens the theme of Jesus' return to the Father. He speaks, while he is still with them, so that the disciples he is leaving behind may find the joy which follows on the fulfillment of the commandment of love. In bearing witness to the world they must, as he, suffer the world's hate. But that is their task, as it was his. The Father will "keep them from the evil one"—surely an echo of the Lord's Prayer (Mt 6: 13).

The disciples will be consecrated in the truth, that is to say, in God's word—the truth that is Jesus' revelation of the unseen God. To be consecrated in the truth means to have a closer union with Jesus, who is the Truth (14: 6). They have accepted him and kept his word (17: 6, 14); now they must bring him and his word to others. Jesus sends them as he himself was sent; the mission of this community of the faith is to continue the mission of Jesus. By his death (his "consecration") Jesus will confirm and consecrate his disciples. His death is a sacrifice, the supreme high-priestly action on their behalf.

Prayer for All

> I do not pray for these only, but also for those who are to
> believe in me through their word, that they may all be one;
> even as thou, Father, art in me, and I in thee, that they also
> may be in us, so that the world may believe that thou hast
> sent me. The glory which thou hast given me I have given
> to them, that they may be one even as we are one, I in them
> and thou in me, that they may become perfectly one, so
> that the world may know that thou hast sent me and hast
> loved them even as thou hast loved me. Father, I desire
> that they also, whom thou hast given me, may be with me
> where I am, to behold my glory which thou hast given me
> in thy love for me before the foundation of the world. O
> righteous Father, the world has not known thee, but I have
> known thee; and these know that thou hast sent me. I have
> made known to them thy name, and I will make it known,
> that the love with which thou hast loved me may be in
> them, and I in them (17: 20-26).

The mission of the disciples will be efficacious, made so
by the prayer of Jesus. The power of his prayer reaches out
to those others, those who will come to "believe into
him"—that is the force of the Greek; for the faith means a
personal relationship with Jesus, union with him. And
Jesus prays for the unity of the community. Unity follows
on the communion of the Christian with Father and Son.
The missionary role is not lost to sight: "that the world
may believe." Those later disciples, like the initial group,
are sent, as the Master was, "to bear witness to the truth"
(18: 37). "Glory" will be theirs as, in their turn and
measure, they make Father and Son known. But they can
have this "Glory," this revealing role, only if they are one
with Father and Son and with one another. Only so will
their witness have force. Only so will it be witness to a God
who is love.

If Jesus had not prayed that his disciples should be taken
out of the world (17: 15) that was in view of their task of
carrying on his work. As he had come into the world to do
the saving will of the Father and, that task accomplished

(19: 30), to return, in glory, to that beloved Father, so he wills and prays that his disciples, when they have accomplished their task, will enjoy unending blessedness with him. Then, for them too, the message they had preached will be wholly clear. They will see, and share in, the perfect union of Father and Son and glow in their love. All will be achieved in and through their being with Jesus, fully and forever. It is because the Father had given them to the Son, and because they had been joined with him on earth, as branches of the Vine, that they will be united with him forever. They are those who have known Father and Son—and that is what eternal life is all about (17: 3).

The closing words of the prayer bring us back to earth. Jesus will make the Father more deeply known. But that will be at the cost of love. It is only in a loving community that the love of Father and Son can be experienced, that Father and Son can be truly known. Only in loving one another can the disciples be one with Jesus; only so will he dwell among them and be in them. It is the earnest prayer of Jesus that this be so: "I pray for them" (17: 20).

Hebrews

A major theme of the Letter to the Hebrews is that of the priesthood of Christ. The coming of the Son into this world is presented in cultic terms. It is almost as if he had come precisely to be our High Priest who offers sacrifice for us (Heb 2: 17; 8: 1-6; 9: 11-14; 10: 1-18) and who intercedes for us.

Hebrews is very insistent on the sheer humanness of our High Priest. "He had to become like his brethren in every respect, so that he might become a merciful and faithful high priest in the service of God, to make expiation for the sins of the people. For because he himself has suffered, he is able to help those who are tempted" (2: 17-18). "We have not a high priest who is unable to sympathize with our weakness, but one who in every respect has been tempted as we are, yet without sinning" (4: 15). "For every high

priest chosen from among men is appointed on behalf of
men in relation to God...So also Christ...although he
was a Son, he learned obedience through what he suffered...." (5: 1, 5, 8). It is not surprising that, as we have
seen earlier, this Jesus should "in the days of his flesh"
pray to and supplicate the Father. Gethsemane is primarily
in view (5: 7), but the implication is clear that Jesus prayed
throughout his earthly life. What interests us here,
however, is his continuing intercession for us in heaven.
While it is of much importance for us that "because he
himself has suffered and been tempted, he is able to help
those who are tempted" (2: 18), it is of greater importance
that he who has "passed through the heavens" (4: 14) has
not forgotten us.

Intercession

> Since then we have a great high priest who has passed
> through the heavens, Jesus, the Son of God, let us hold
> fast our confession. For we have not a high priest who is
> unable to sympathize with our weakness, but one who in
> every respect has been tempted as we are, yet without sin-
> ning. Let us then with confidence draw near to the throne
> of grace, that we may receive mercy and find grace to help
> in time of need (Heb 4: 14-16).

The fact that Jesus the high priest has entered the
heavenly sanctuary (6: 20; 7: 26; 8: 1; 9: 11) is a motive for
holding fast to the faith we confess. Verse 15 is a reply to a
latent objection; may not this surprising greatness of the
high priest imply an aloofness toward human misery.
"Sympathize" here means to sympathize in the sense of
entering into and sharing the sufferings of others. We need
have no fear. Our high priest can sympathize with us in our
temptations; he can help us because he has experienced our
trials and sufferings. Having such a high priest—now
passed into the presence of God, remember—Christians
can advance with full confidence to present themselves
before God. The "throne of grace" is the throne of God's

mercy. It is because it is now accessible to sinners that it is the throne of grace; the way of access is Christ the Priest, the link between God and mankind. Christians who approach the throne encounter the loving mercy of God who bestows on them his favours.

Our high priest has attained his rest (cf 3: 7-4: 13) and through him we have access to the mercy and grace of God. He has entered into heaven but he is united to us still by his perfect understanding of our trials and difficulties. The distance between us, abolished by the incarnation, has not been broadened again by the ascension. He is always ready and able to help us because he is always our compassionate high priest.

A feature of Hebrews is a contrast between the transitory priesthood of the priests of Israel and the unique and unending priesthood of Christ.

> He holds his priesthood permanently, because he continues forever. Consequently he is able for all time to save those who draw near to God through him, since he always lives to make intercession for them (7: 24-25).

The mission of the Son is to bring men to God. In heaven, he carries out unceasingly his priestly ministry. No longer, of course, the ministry of sacrifice: his supremely efficacious sacrifice was offered once for all (9: 28; 10: 10). But he does exercise the priestly ministry of intercession. He is our sympathetic and confident advocate.

> Christ has entered, not into a sanctuary made with hands, a copy of the true one, but into heaven itself, now to appear in the presence of God on our behalf (9: 24).

The background to this statement is the annual Israelite ritual of the Day of Atonement (Lev 16; Heb 9). The high priest, on this day of the year, entered the holy of holies (the "sanctuary made with hands") to offer the blood of the expiatory sacrifice. But Christ has come to no man-made sanctuary, and he has made no futile offering of the "blood of goats and bulls" (Heb 9: 13). He has entered, once for all, the heavenly Holy Place, by virtue of his own blood shed in sacrifice. The purpose of his heavenly ministry is to appear in God's presence on our behalf. His role as heavenly priest is, now and forever, to plead on our behalf. He pleads by his efficacious presence as the Son who had been given by God for the world's sake (cf Jn 3: 16) and who had returned to the Father, having accomplished the task of reconciliation.

> Therefore, brethren, since we have confidence to enter the sanctuary by the blood of Jesus...let us draw near with a true heart in full assurance of faith (10: 19, 22).

The "blood of Jesus" is a symbol for the saving achievement of Jesus (9: 12, 22; 12: 24). That sacrificial blood is eloquent. We who have been washed clean by him can come to the "heavenly Jerusalem," can come "to Jesus, the mediator of a new covenant, and to the sprinkled blood that speaks more graciously than the blood of Abel" (12: 22-24). The blood of Abel had cried out for vengeance (Gen 4: 10). The blood of Jesus speaks reconciliation. It is a voice that will not be stilled. We can come, with a true and confident heart, to the Father of love.

If we could but hear this wondrous, this comforting "word of exhortation" (Heb 13: 22) what might it not do for our prayer. Who could not rush to the embrace of such a Father and such a Brother! Our trouble is that we do not listen.

Nine

Teach Us to Pray

Jesus prayed to God—there is no doubt about that. We have seen, clearly enough, that we have so much to learn about prayer from the prayers of the children of Israel. But, in Jesus, we are up against the unique. Here is a son of Israel who is also Son of God. John, predictably, has caught the implication: "No one has ever seen God; the only son, who is in the bosom of the Father, he has made him known" (Jn 1: 18). If we are to pray as we ought it can only be because we have listened to this Son who is alert to the Father. And if we are disciples of the Son we will ask, as his first disciples did, "Lord, teach us to pray" (Lk 11: 1).

What did he teach? We do not need to plow through learned tomes. What Jesus had to say about prayer is not something that can be confined between the covers of a book. His own life was prayer and his words of prayer fit snugly within his life. He has taught us to pray out of our day-to-day life. He has taught us to pray with confidence and perseveringly. He has asked us, simply, to pray as children of God to a God who is our Father.

Jesus believed in prayer; his own practice made that manifest. And he lost no opportunity of speaking of prayer to his disciples and the crowds. It was so natural for him to turn to the Father that he wanted all men and women to converse freely with a God whom they might and should address confidently as "Abba"—Daddy.

Matthew and Luke have each made a synthesis of Jesus' teaching on prayer, the one in a grouping of sayings, the other in a collection of parables.

MATTHEW

In the heart of the Sermon on the Mount (chs 5-7), Matthew has Jesus recommend to his disciples the traditional Jewish good works of almsgiving, prayer and fasting—but without ostentation. One can readily see that, originally, the passage was made up of the three units 6: 2-4, 5-6, 16-18—the uniform construction of the units makes that much clear. It is obvious that Matthew took advantage of the reference to prayer here to fill out the teaching of Jesus on the subject (6: 7-15).

> And when you pray, you must not be like the hypocrites; for they love to stand and pray in the synagogues and at the street corners, that they may be seen by men. Truly, I say to you, they have their reward. But when you pray, go into your room and shut the door and pray to your Father who is in secret; and your Father who sees in secret will reward you (Mt 6: 5-6).

A firm anti-Pharisee bias runs through Matthew. It reflects the historical situation after the destruction of Jerusalem in 70 A.D., the reorganization of a shattered Judaism during which the separation of synagogue and church became definitive. More immediately, "the Pharisees" represent a legalistic element within Matthew's community. "And when you pray": it is assumed that Christians will pray. What is in question is how they ought to pray—or, in the first instance, how they ought not pray. They must not make a spectacle of prayer. What is in question is motivation rather than actual practice. Prayer in

public can be edifying. One cannot fail to be impressed by
the piety of a Muslim workman who quietly spreads his
mat high on a building scaffold and prays to his God. This
is not ostentation; it is touching faith. Our passage has in
mind rather the professional—cleric or religious—who is
indecently pious. Prayer, Jesus insists, is primarily an affair between oneself and God—a child talking with his
Father. He will, of course, in another context, firmly remind the individual that he is one of a family, remind him
that all God's children are equally dear to him and that he
expects them to love one another and pray together.

> And in praying do not heap up empty phrases as the Gen-
> tiles do; for they think that they will be heard for their
> many words. Do not be like them, for your Father knows
> what you need before you ask him (6: 7-8).

Another negative precept, but this time in view of Gentile practice. Invocation of pagan deities was regularly a
fulsome affair. The gods' attention had to be attracted,
hence a prelude of elaborate titles and adulatory attributes.
There is no need for any of this when one turns, trustfully,
to an Abba. A child does not set out to flatter his Daddy.
Besides, this Father is more keenly aware of the needs of
his children than they themselves are. One does not need to
shout to attract his attention. It might seem that nothing
could be clearer than this admonition of the Lord. Prayer
is to be simple and direct; it is not to be longwinded. The
sad fact is that Christian practice has been so different.
And here one cannot lay the blame at the door of the "simple faithful." Here it is the professionals who have been
glaringly at fault. I do sympathize with the nostalgia of
some Catholics for the "old church." I sympathize—but I
am so glad to be free of that past. I am glad for many
reasons, and one of them lies just here. We had heaped up
"empty phrases," we religious and priests. We "prayed,"
interminably, in a dead language—for some in a language
they did not know. And this prayer was turned into a grim
duty, an obligation to be carried out under pain of grave

sin. Jesus had bidden us; "When you pray, say: Abba" (Lk 11: 2). We had not heard. We had not taken him at his word.

These negative rulings had cleared the way for the positive teaching of the Lord: "Pray then like this." We will study the Lord's Prayer (Mt 6: 9-13) later in the chapter. Here we would note only the insistence on forgiveness (v 12) underlined by the addition of vv 14-15. This, we have suggested, sets the admonition to prayer in secret in its proper perspective. Even when alone we are never forgetful of belonging to the family of God.

LUKE

The third evangelist finds Jesus' teaching on prayer in his parables: perseverance in prayer (Lk 11: 5-13; 18: 1-8) and humility in praying (18: 9-14). Yet, quite like Matthew, he has in the context of the Lord's Prayer (11: 2-4) built up a synthesis of teaching on prayer: the parable (11: 5-8) and the assurance that prayer will be heard (11: 9-13).

The parable of the Importunate Friend (11: 5-8) is, in its Lucan setting, addressed to the disciples who had asked to be taught how to pray (11: 1). Jesus did teach them his prayer and then went on to a further lesson:

> Which of you who has a friend will go to him at midnight and say to him, "Friend, lend me three loaves; for a friend of mine has arrived on a journey, and I have nothing to set before him"; and he will answer from within, "Do not bother me; the door is now shut, and my children are with me in bed; I cannot get up and give you anything"? I tell you, though he will not get up and give him anything because he is his friend, yet because of his importunity he will rise and give him whatever he needs (11: 5-8).

Originally, in the setting of Jesus' ministry, the parable would have made its point through the conduct of the one who is being importuned. The phrase "which of you" means "Can you imagine that you would act so?" and invites an indignant "Of course not!" In that case, Jesus tells his hearers, you cannot imagine that God will reject the plea of one who calls upon him. With the suggestion that God might in any way be like this boor ("Do not bother me") we are in the line of that daring familiarity of the Old Testament.

In Luke's setting the focus is on the one who pleads. He has come, in need, to a friend. The situation was urgent. A friend had called on him, unexpectedly, and he *must* be given hospitality. The other friend, though roused from sleep at midnight, ought to have appreciated the gravity of the situation. In the interest of the story he shows himself insensitive to the normal eastern feeling for the claim of hospitality. Very well, let the pleader keep up his pestering; he will be given what he wants if only to be rid of him! When we recall that this is a teaching on prayer to God we can savour, also in this new setting, the daring of it. Even when the emphasis is switched to perseverance, the implication is still there that God is one who must be worn down. Jeremiah and Job would be at home with this parable. And the Christian must take heart from the fact that the Lord could present such a visage of the Father, if only to insist that he is wholly other.

Luke is concerned about perseverance in prayer. He has another parable, markedly like to one we have seen, with the same message (18: 2-8). He has spelt out his intent: "And he told them a parable to the effect that they ought always to pray and not lose heart" (18: 1).

> In a certain city there was a judge who neither feared God nor regarded man; and there was a widow in that city who kept coming to him and saying, "Vindicate me against my adversary." For a while he refused; but afterward he said to himself, "Though I neither fear God nor regard man, yet because this widow bothers me, I will vindicate her, or she will wear me out by her continual coming." And the Lord said, "Hear what the unrighteous judge says. And will not God vindicate his elect, who cry to him day and

night? Will he delay long over them? I tell you, he will vindicate them speedily. Nevertheless, when the Son of man comes, will he find faith on earth?" (18: 2-8).

As before, Jesus would have asked his hearers to contemplate, if they would, a God cast in the image of this unjust judge. Could they really imagine that he was remotely like that? It is the widow who holds Luke's attention—with the bonus that he has now balanced his male-role parable (11: 5-8) with this female-role parable. (Note the twin parables, 15: 3-7, 8-10.) The widow, aware that she cannot pay the bribe expected by this venal judge, has no recourse but to pester. If she makes enough of a nuisance of herself he will grant her request merely for the sake of peace and quiet. What a bold picture of prayer to God this is! The parable is rounded off by an *a fortiori*. If this cynical judge will, in the end, yield to the importunity of the persistent widow, surely it is to be expected that God who is not a judge at all, but a loving Father, will yield to the importunity of his children! No, he will not delay. As always, the problem is not with the constant God; it is with his inconstant creature. Is there the faith that will support this confident and persevering prayer? Each Christian must answer for herself or himself.

The other parable of the Pharisee and the Tax Collector (18: 9-14) does fit neatly into the ministry of Jesus. Both characters are drawn from life: the righteous one and the outcast. And the parable is spoken as a warning to the righteous: "He also told this parable to some who trusted in themselves that they were righteous and despised others" (18: 9).

> Two men went up into the temple to pray, one a Pharisee and the other a tax collector. The Pharisee stood and prayed thus with himself, "God, I thank thee that I am not like other men, extortioners, unjust, adulterers, or even like this tax collector. I fast twice a week, I give tithes of all that I get." But the tax collector, standing far off, would not even lift up his eyes to heaven, but beat his breast, saying, "God, be merciful to me a sinner!" I tell you, this man

went down to his house justified rather than the other [i.e.
the other was not heard]; for every one who exalts himself
will be humbled, but he who humbles himself will be exalted. (18: 10-14).

So often the Pharisee of this parable has been called a
hypocrite. It is an error which clouds the pathos of the
parable and blunts its impact. The sad fact is that the man
is sincere and his claims are true. He is scrupulously
honest, a faithful family man, a meticulous observer of the
Law (as the tax-collector by definition is not). The Law en-
joined only one fast a year (on the Day of Atonement) but
he, a pious Pharisee, fasts each Monday and Thursday.
And, far beyond the demands of the Law, he gives tithes of
all his possessions. He is sincerely convinced that he stands
right with God. After all, he has done what he ought to do,
and more. He can truly thank God that he is not like other
men. The snag is that his "prayer" is not prayer at all. That
is why it is not heard.

It is this sort of person and this attitude Paul has in mind
in Galatians and Romans. He had seen with clarity (for he,
too, had been a convinced Pharisee) that one for whom the
heart of religion is observance may feel that he can earn
salvation. What he must avoid and must do are clear to
him. If he is faithful, then a just God cannot but justify
him. He cannot understand that salvation is gift. That is
why the Pharisee could not recognize God's gracious gift
in Jesus. And it is because the "sinner" had no such illu-
sions that he could instinctively see the gift for what it was.
There is nothing mysterious in the fact that Jesus was a
"friend of tax collectors and sinners," nor that this was
scandal to the "righteous."

There is a wry point to the story about the good lady
who, after a Sunday morning homily on our parable, was
heard to remark: "Thank God I am not like that
Pharisee!" For "pharisaism" is not only a late Jewish
phenomenon. It is endemic to the Christian church and has
proved a hardy growth. The self-righteous Christian is not
a rarity. Regular church-going and certain pious practices

may seem to set one apart and guarantee salvation. Always, of course, it is a case of "these you ought to have done, without neglecting the others"—but the "weightier matters" of justice, mercy and faith are what religion is all about (Mt 23: 23-24).

The tax collector was a man bereft of hope, though not without faith. He had been robbed of hope by the righteous, so thoroughly branded an outcast that he had come to regard himself as such. If salvation depended on meticulous observance of the Law, as the Pharisees maintained, then he had no chance at all. But he cannot bring himself to believe that God is like that. Hoping against hope, he dared to come to the temple of God. And his prayer is the most moving of all prayers. It is a prayer that should sound an echo in our hearts, a prayer that should spring, unbidden, to our lips. "God, be merciful to me a sinner." What a marvelous example of the prayer that answers to the warning: "And in praying do not heap up empty phrases" (Mt 6: 7). This is the prayer that God listens to and answers—"this man went down to his house justified." The second half of verse 14 ("for every one who exalts himself will be humbled, and he who humbles himself will be exalted", explicitly lifts this parable out of the ministry of Jesus, away from any narrow conflict of Pharisee and tax collector, and turns it into a lesson for Everyman.

Empty Words

We have looked at "prayer" that is not prayer at all. There is prayer that is insincere. It is prayer to God, but it is not matched by concern for God and his ways.

> Not every one who says to me, "Lord, Lord," shall enter the kingdom of heaven, but he who does the will of my Father who is in heaven (Mt 7: 21).

Or, as Luke puts it, more succinctly:

> Why do you call me, "Lord, Lord," and do not do what I
> tell you (Lk 6: 46).

Confession of Jesus as "Lord" is a profession of faith. It
is acknowledgment of his lordship; it is prayer of praise
and adoration. But if, afterwards, we do not do what he
asks of us, it is an empty phrase. If Jesus is truly my Lord,
I owe him faithful service. If I do not serve, I am living a
lie.

Confident Prayer

A living faith means confidence in prayer:

> Therefore I tell you, whatever you ask in prayer, believe
> that you receive it, and you will (Mk 11: 24; cf Mt 21: 21).

In authentically Semitic fashion, Jesus had underlined the
message with striking hyperbole: "Truly, I say to you,
whoever says to this mountain, 'Be taken up and cast into
the sea,' and does not doubt in his heart, but believes that
what he says will come to pass, it will be done for him" (Mk
11: 23; cf Mt 21: 21). Faith is meant to be a living, and a
lived, faith. It is the opposite of the insincerity we have
noted. It is the quality of faith of a justified tax collector.
Having experienced the mercy he had pleaded for, he will,
we may be sure, commit himself to this merciful God—a
powerful God, who can move mountains; how much more
readily the molehills of human worry. All that is needed is
to trust him, implicitly. Paul had got the message: "I can
do all things in him who strengthens me" (Phil 4: 13).

It Will Be Given

The confident prayer that springs from a lived faith will
be heard.

> Ask, and it will be given you; seek, and you will find;
> knock, and it will be opened to you. For every one who

asks receives, and he who seeks finds, and to him who
knocks it will be opened. Or what man of you, if his son
asks him for bread, will give him a stone? Or if he asks for
a fish will give him a serpent? If you then, who are evil,
know how to give good gifts to your children, how much
more will your Father who is in heaven give good things to
those who ask him! (Mt 7: 7-11; cf Lk 11: 9-13).

Ask...seek...knock...Can we square this exhortation
with the assurance that "your Father knows what you need
before you ask him" (Mt 6: 8)? Readily. God does not
need us; he does not need our prayer. But we do need him;
we need to acknowledge our dependence on him.
"Dependence" can be a dirty word; in human society it is,
too often, a filthy word. But, in a context of creature and
Creator, dependence can have another meaning. The
creature MAN is the closest creature to God in God's creation. As creature, he depends on his Creator. We may, in
human conduct, find a key to an understanding of his
dependence. There is the dependence of an infant on its
mother. When this is instinct with love, as it is meant to be,
it is a thing of beauty. It is heartening to see how, for instance, in bus or train or plane, the sight of a young
mother absorbed in the gurgling tot in her arms wins spontaneous smiles and nods. That babe is revelling in
dependence! And the mother is certainly not domineering.
It is a simple fact of life. The infant is wholly dependent,
there is no escaping the fact. And *only* in the acceptance of
dependence can the child hope to grow to the maturity of
manhood or womanhood.

It is quite the same with humankind in relation to God.
We are, whether we will or not, God's creatures, dependent on him. And only in relation to our God can we
become fully human. We must acknowledge our
dependence; we must ask and seek and knock. The need is
ours, not his. And the answer will be his. The analogy of
mother and child can help us again. A loving mother
knows what is good and best for her child. He may ask,
may demand; but she will give only what is helpful. A firm

"no" is often the most loving answer. A loving Father will give, will open the way—but only when it is best. We should not forget that "No" is quite as much an answer as "Yes"—even to prayer!

The human analogy, of course, breaks down. A father will not give a live snake or a venomous scorpion to his child who asks for bread. The Father's giving, on the contrary, will, often enough, appear hurtful. At first, his fish and egg may seem to be serpent and scorpion. We may well ask, "Why did God do this to me?" But where there is faith and littleness it will, in time, be clear that his gift is always goodness. Significantly, Luke has transformed the original text. The "good things" of the Father's giving (Mt 7: 11) have become the gift *par excellence*, source of all goodness: "how much more will the heavenly Father give the Holy Spirit to those who ask him" (Lk 11: 13). The Holy Spirit, God's supreme gift, is the answer to our deepest prayer.

Gathered in My Name

Prayer is a matter of the individual and his God, an intimate chat between child and Father. But children can, and do, as a group, importune their parents. Christians, too, may and should pray together to their Father.

> Again I say to you, if two of you agree on earth about anything they ask, it will be done for them by my Father in heaven. For where two or three are gathered in my name, there am I in the midst of them (Mt 18: 19-20).

A prayer acceptable to God is one which is in accord with what is best for his child. Nothing can please him more than when two of his children acknowledge their family bond in turning to him together. Then, there is the further comforting assurance, reaching beyond the unhappy rifts in the body of Christendom. When Christians meet, as Christians, the Lord is there among them. This must surely be so when they meet to further harmony and brotherhood. Yet how deaf we had been to this assurance of the Lord. It is not long ago at all when Roman Catholics were explicitly forbidden to pray together with their Christian brethren. *We* had decided who the true disciples of the Lord were. We knew that we were "not like other men." Happily, the Holy Spirit has his ways of dealing with human blindness. And, through Vatican II, he stirred us to acknowledge our brethren and their churches. The Lord of peace is certainly there where Christians meet in sincere ecumenism.

The Harvest

The great commission of the Risen Lord to his disciples had been: "Go and make disciples of all nations" (Mt 29: 19). It is a task that will challenge Christians while this world lasts. Indeed, we see the harvest-field grow wider and more lush decade by decade. The Lord had foreseen the growth and the need.

> The harvest is plentiful, but the labourers are few; pray therefore the Lord of the harvest to send out labourers into the harvest (Mt 9: 37; Lk 10: 2).

Matthew has this saying in a setting of Jesus' expressed compassion for crowds helpless without a shepherd to guide them (Mt 9: 35-36). That compassion of the Lord reaches out still to the harassed and helpless of the world. Luke has the saying in the context of the sending out of the seventy-two (Lk 10: 1-12)—already foreshadowing the universal Christian mission.

Today, we must not lose heart. The task seems hopeless, in face of a population explosion and a dwindling band of harvesters. What can *we* do! This job is too big for us. We must not give in, if we are to count ourselves Christian. Despondency comes because we forget the true meaning and the real power of Christianity. We are not alone. Our trouble is that we will get in the way of the Spirit of the Lord. And, of course, we need to be convinced of our

Christian obligation to bear witness. We can pray, with fervor and perseverance to the Lord of the harvest, beseeching him to raise up worthy harvesters, only if we are first aware of the need and of our duty. The commission is for all; the call to prayer is to all. And the Lord did not require that his harvesters be celibate!

Forgiveness

In his parable of The Servant Without Mercy (Mt 18: 23-35) Jesus had made a demand, had made it with sternness. One who owed an immense debt (twenty million dollars) sought mercy and made a plea of desperation, impossible of fulfillment, that he would repay in full. With unheard-of generosity, the king simply wrote off the debt. Behind servant and king stand the sinner and his God. Then the glaring contrast on the human level. One who had met with such mercy could not find it in his heart to be generous toward his fellowman. His conduct angered the king. Jesus insists that a good God who will readily forgive the most heinous offences will not tolerate a failing in mercy. The fate of that hard-hearted man stands as a salutary warning: "So also my heavenly Father will do to every one of you, if you do not forgive your brother from your heart" (Mt 18: 35). A demand that Jesus makes, relentlessly and repeatedly, is the demand of forgiveness. He does so with insistence because of the truth that a Christian is one who has met with unstinted forgiveness.

It is no surprise, then, that Jesus linked prayer and forgiveness:

> Whenever you stand praying, forgive, if you have anything against anyone; so that your Father also who is in heaven may forgive you your trespasses (Mk 11: 25).

An unforgiving spirit raises a barrier to mercy. It is an aspect of Paul's doctrine of justification by faith. Salvation is a gift, freely and lovingly offered. The only proviso is that one be willing to receive. And one who will not extend mercy does not recognize mercy for what it is. Or, to put it another way, one who will not forgive has not understood God's forgiveness—has not really known God. And how can one truly pray to a God one does not know?

In Matthew that admonition of Jesus takes the sterner form of a grim warning. It occurs as a codicil to the Lord's Prayer, a commentary on the petition: "And forgive us our debts, as we also have forgiven our debtors" (Mt 6: 12).The implication is that we are expected to forgive others before we plead for God's forgiveness of us. Indeed (as the prayer stands) we make our forgiveness of others a condition of God's forgiveness of us. The commentary simply makes unmistakable the sense of the petition: "For if you forgive men their trespasses, your heavenly Father also will forgive you; if you do not forgive men their trespasses, neither will your Father forgive your trespasses" (6: 14-15). The obligation of forgiveness cannot be stressed any more clearly. Well for us it is that God is God and not man (cf Hos 11: 9). He does not really temper his boundless mercy to our grudging forgiveness. But what he expects of us is clear. We may assume that the tax collector of the parable who, to his wonderment, has met a merciful God, would henceforth rejoice in forgiving those who might injure him. So it should be with every child of God.

Love Your Enemy

Jesus makes one demand more, a demand that breaks the limit of human conduct:

> I say to you, love your enemies and pray for those who persecute you (Mt 5: 44).

Luke fills out the demand and makes clear that its range is universal:

> I say to you that hear, Love your enemies, do good to those
> who hate you, bless those who curse you, pray for those
> who abuse you (Lk 6: 27-28).

This is revolutionary. If Christians have never really
been able to live up to the one commandment ("Love one
another"), it goes without saying that they have failed,
miserably, to heed this hard saying. For hard saying undoubtedly it is. But it is a demand of the Lord. The enemy
of the Christian is also a child of God: one to whom God
holds out the gift of salvation, one from whom God will
not withhold forgiveness if there be an opening for his
mercy. Pray for those who abuse and persecute. The world
will respond with scorn, for this is folly. Of course it is: it
has about it a touch of the foolishness of the cross. And
that is why it is an authentically Christian course.

The Lord's Prayer

> He was praying in a certain place, and when he ceased, one
> of his disciples said to him, "Lord teach us to pray, as John
> taught his disciples" (Lk 11: 1).

Luke has provided a wholly credible setting for the
Lord's Prayer. It is not only that the disciples were,
understandably, taken by the mien of Jesus in prayer to the
Father. They had come to see themselves as a group apart,
a group, in their own eyes, as distinctive as that of the
followers of the Baptist. It was time for them to have their
very own prayer. And that prayer will remain, for all time,
the characteristic prayer of disciples of Jesus.

Matthew (6: 9-13) and Luke (11: 2-4) have given two
versions of the prayer. The first, obvious, difference is that
Matthew's form is the longer. More importantly, Matthew
has preserved the original strongly eschatological flavour
of it, while Luke has adapted it to fit the modest pattern of
day-by-day Christian living.

> Our Father who art in heaven.
> Hallowed be thy name,

> Thy kingdom come,
> Thy will be done,
> on earth as it is in heaven,
> give us this day our daily bread;
> And forgive us our debts,
> as we also have forgiven our debtors;
> and lead us not into temptation,
> but deliver us from evil (Mt 6: 9-13).

The first three petitions really boil down to the central one: Thy kingdom come. The use of the passive tense is a conventional way of indicating an action of God. We call upon the Father in heaven to manifest his holiness, to show forth his saving will by bringing about his glorious Reign. The petition, "give us today our daily bread" very likely should read: "Give us today our bread of the morrow," that is to say, the bread of the heavenly banquet—the bread of the Kingdom. The plea for the forgiveness of all sin ("debts") also looks to the end, when Sin will be no more. And we pray not to be crushed by the great Temptation, the End-time crisis, to escape, at last, and forever, the designs of the Evil One. From first to last it is a prayer of faith and hope, a prayer that looks firmly beyond this world to the Reign of the Father.

It was a prayer that would spring readily to the lips of our first brethren, who looked to the imminent return of their Lord.

> Father,
> hallowed be thy name.
> Thy kingdom come.
> Give us each day our daily bread;
> and forgive us our sins,
> for we ourselves forgive every one who is
> indebted to us;
> and lead us not into temptation (Lk 11: 2-4).

Luke's simpler "Father" (in place of the solemn "Our Father who art in heaven" of Matthew) represents the intimate *Abba* of Jesus' own address to his Father. He calls on his disciples to come to their Father in the same uninhibited manner. "Give us each day our daily bread" is a child-like request for the ordinary needs of life. Christians, even as they do look to a goal beyond earthly confines, must yet steadfastly live out their lives in the only world they know. They have need of the concern and the care of One who will care for them. The Father who arrays the lilies of the field and feeds the birds will not neglect his children (Mt 6: 25-33; Lk 12: 22-31). The disturbing truth is that daily bread is not for all and that little ones do go in need. But is this because we have not taken the whole message to heart: "But seek first his kingdom and his righteousness, and all these things shall be yours as well" (Mt 6: 33)? Chesterton may have had the right of it when he remarked that Christianity had not failed—because it had never been tried. Luke has softened the Semitic starkness of the call to forgiveness. It remains, for him, an inescapable obligation: "forgive...for we ourselves forgive." Do we can we sincerely pray this prayer? An honest answer will tell us something of the quality of our Christianity.

Ten

Prayer to Jesus

Jesus has shown us a loving Father and has invited us to turn to the Father with simplicity and candor. That being so, how could the disciples, beyond cross-and-resurrection, have turned to him in any other way when they had come to know that he was Son of God. How could they turn in any other way than the way he had taught them to turn to the Father—now colored by the ineffable experience of their meeting with him. He had shown them the Father in a new light. Now they saw their Jesus in a fresh blaze of light.

"You are the Messiah" (Mk 8: 29). That first faltering confession of Peter was so wide of the reality (cf 8: 31-33). Only when one has come to terms with the cross can one truly confess the Lord. That is Mark's message, and it is also word of Paul. It is word of the New Testament. Paradoxically, to accept the cross of Jesus, is already to acknowledge him as Son of God.

"My Lord and my God" (Jn 20: 28). These words of Thomas are the most solemn profession of Christian faith in our gospels. They are sublime, that goes without saying. But Mark has alerted us to a danger. Confession is not enough. Jesus himself had warned us: it is not enough to cry out "Lord, Lord." One has to do more than call out, one has to live the way of the Lord (cf Mt 7: 22-23). There is no escaping the truth that the Christian way is Way. Our discipleship is proved by our living. Our Christian prayer is proved by whether or not it is the inspiration and the sustenance of our walking the Christian way.

In the light of the resurrection the disciples clearly discerned, for the first time, the uniqueness of Jesus. He was God's Son in a way that no other had been a son of God. Step by step, not logically but intuitively, the early Christians worked out the implications of their discernment and built their Christology (the theological understanding of Jesus). At first they regarded the resurrection as the decisive moment, the key to the meaning of Jesus. Acts is formal: God raised up Jesus and made him Lord and Christ (2: 32-36); God, at the resurrection, exalted him as Leader and Saviour (5: 30-31); Jesus was begotten as God's Son through the resurrection (13: 32-33; cf Rom 1: 3-4). A later stage, reflected in Mark, shows an awareness that the Lord Jesus Christ was Son of God from the moment of baptism. "Thou art my beloved Son" (Mk 1: 11)—was Son of God throughout his ministry. Yet this is not enough. In the infancy gospels of Matthew and Luke (Mt 1-2; Lk 1-2) the understanding of Jesus as Messiah, Son of David, Saviour and Lord is pushed back to the infancy period; he is Lord not only through resurrection, not only during his ministry, but also from the beginning of his earthly existence. The final step was one to pre-existence and incarnation. This is reached in John: "In the beginning was the Word, and the Word was with God, and the Word was God...and the Word became flesh..." (Jn 1: 1, 14).

The development—surely not as neat as we have presented it—was no more than a theological working-out of an understanding of the status of Jesus, which was there from the start. It followed that prayer could be addressed to Jesus. Our gospels were written in communities with decades of Christian living and tradition behind them. Christian understanding colors even the presentation of the ministry of Jesus. It is undoubtedly true that many in their need had come to Jesus to ask for his compassion and his help. In that asking, Christians had discerned overtones of their own prayer to the Lord. The synoptic gospels, too, can teach us about prayer to him.

At an early stage in the ministry Jesus visited Simon Peter's home at Capernaum, to find Simon's mother-in-law prostrate with fever—"Now Simon's mother-in-law was ill with a high fever, and they besought him for her" (Lk 4: 38). When Jesus "rebuked" the fever, it left her and she got up to serve him and his disciples. Later disciples might well have seen in the incident a symbolic portrayal of the believer: one formerly spiritually ill, now, through prayer to Jesus and by his power, restored to health and summoned to serve him.

Have Mercy on Me

Prayer, and answer to prayer, figure in the healing of a leper:

> And a leper came to him, beseeching him, and kneeling said to him, "If you will, you can make me clean." Moved with pity, he stretched out his hand and said to him, "I will; be clean." And immediately the leprosy left him, and he was made clean (Mk 1: 40-42; cf Lk 5: 12; Mt 8: 2).

Leprosy (a term which in the Bible covers a variety of diseases) was regarded as the ultimate uncleanness which cut one off from the community, which put one outside the pale. And it is to be noted that, after his healing, the former leper began "to spread the news"—or, as it might just as well be rendered, "to proclaim the word." The deeper meaning of the incident is not hard to find: the Christian is one who through appeal to Christ is "cleansed" by him in baptism, one who then ought to "preach" and "spread abroad the Good News."

A moving passage in Mark is that about the blind man at Jericho (Mk 10: 46-52). Jesus, with his disciples, was on the way to Jerusalem. A blind man, who sat begging outside the town gate, heard the commotion and was told that Jesus of Nazareth was passing by.

> He began to cry out and say, "Jesus, Son of David, have mercy on me!" And many rebuked him telling him to be silent; but he cried out all the more, "Son of David, have mercy on me!" And Jesus stopped and said, "Call him." And they called the blind man, saying to him, "Take heart; rise, he is calling you." And throwing off his mantle he sprang up and came to Jesus. And Jesus said to him, "What do you want me to do for you?" And the blind man said to him, "Master, let me receive my sight." And Jesus said to him, "Go your way; your faith has made you well." And immediately he received his sight and followed him on the way (Mk 10: 47-52; cf Lk 18: 35-43; Mt 20: 29-34).

This narrative focuses on the blind man who is thereby presented as a model of faith in Jesus in spite of discouragement, and as one who eagerly answers the call of the Master and follows him in the way of discipleship. Jesus challenges the man to make his request (v 51). His request is simple and humble; he is conscious of his need and of his helplessness and finds his only hope in Jesus' nearness. And Jesus responds to his need: "your faith has made you well"—he was healed because he trusted in the power of God manifest in Jesus. "Made you well" can equally well be translated "saved you." The Christian is one who turns to Jesus in faithful prayer and wins salvation. Enlightened by Jesus, he can walk the way of discipleship with confidence.

Faith

Jesus demands faith of those who come to him, beseeching him. This is so in the case of the two blind men who followed him, crying aloud, "Have mercy on us, Son of David" (Mt 9: 27). Jesus asked them, "Do you believe that I am able to do this?" They said to him, "Yes, Lord." Then he touched their eyes, saying, "According to your faith be it done to you." And their eyes were opened. This aspect is more fully developed in the story of Jairus.

> Then came one of the rulers of the synagogue, Jairus by name; and seeing him he fell at his [Jesus'] feet and besought him, saying, "My little daughter is at the point of death. Come and lay your hands on her, so that she may be made well and live." And he went with him (Mk 5: 22-24).

It is obvious that the distraught father sought the cure of his little daughter. At the later catechetical level of the story his prayer would have sounded, "that she may be saved and have (eternal) life!" The Greek words used could not fail to carry that deeper resonance for Christian readers. As the story unfolds, we learn that the girl died and that messengers came to inform Jairus (5: 35). Jesus presents this development as a further challenge to the faith of the father: "Do not fear, only believe" (v 36). Jairus' faith was not misplaced. Jesus came to the room where the child lay, lifeless. "Taking her by the hand he said to her, 'Talitha cumi'; which means, 'Little girl, I say to you, arise.' And immediately the girl got up and walked" (5: 41-42). The verbs "arise" and "got up" are used of the resurrection of Jesus. By inference, he is "the resurrection and the life" (Jn 11: 25). Inserted into the episode of the daughter of Jairus is that of the woman who had come to Jesus in hidden and silent supplication, seeking only to touch his cloak (5: 24-34). She, too, receives the assurance: Daughter, your faith has made you well [has saved you] (5: 34).

Faith comes to fulfillment only in personal encounters with Jesus, only when one enters into dialogue with him. Jairus believed that Jesus had power to heal one at the point of death, when all earthly means had failed. But Jesus looked for a deeper faith: faith in him as one who could raise from the dead, a faith that must find expression in the midst of unbelief. The woman, too, had faith in the power of Jesus. She, too, is asked to have a deeper, fuller faith in him; she meets his gaze and comes to kneel at his feet. And through faith in Jesus she and the little girl are saved. The lesson cannot be missed. The Christian is invited to recognize that one must come to Jesus, seek him out. One must kneel at his feet, not abjectly, but in the intensity of one's pleading (v 22) or in thankfulness (v 33). This Jesus will give to him who believes that peace which the world cannot give (v 34). He will assure him of life beyond death (v 41).

Thanksgiving

There ought to be a response to the answer to our prayer. The story of the ten lepers makes that point with all due emphasis. Here Luke is at his best. The passage speaks for itself and Jesus' disappointment is palpable. Which of us must not, in honesty, line up with the nine? We Christians have known such mercy that we take that mercy for granted, as of right. But that is the way of pharisaism. Luke would have us see that "those outside": centurion (7: 2-10), sinner (7: 36-50), tax collector (19: 1-10), Samaritan (10: 29-37; 17: 11-19), are so much closer to God than the "righteous." They know what mercy is because they know the need of mercy.

> On the way to Jerusalem he was passing along between Samaria and Galilee. And as he entered a village, he was met by ten lepers, who stood at a distance and lifted up their voices and said, "Jesus, Master, have mercy on us." When he saw them he said to them, "Go and show yourselves to the priests." And as they went they were cleansed. Then one of them, when he saw that he was healed, turned back, praising God with a loud voice; and he fell on his face at Jesus' feet, giving him thanks. Now he was a Samaritan. Then said Jesus, "Were not ten cleansed? Where are the nine? Was no one found to return and give praise to God except this foreigner?" And he said to him, "Rise and go your way; your faith has made you well" (Lk 17: 11-19).

One who accepted, as a free and generous gift, the blessing of salvation should not delay to give thanks.

Intercession

Already, the episode of the paralytic (Mk 2: 1-12) had brought out the important factor of the efficacy of prayer on behalf of others. For, indeed, the eloquent gesture of the determined four who dug through a roof in order to get a sick man into Jesus' presence was plea enough! And Jesus accepted it as such: "And when Jesus saw *their* faith..." (v 5). The healing of an epileptic boy was at the earnest behest of his father (Mk 9: 17-29; cf Mt 17: 14-20; Lk 9: 38-43)—as in the case of Jairus and his daughter. But this incident of the epileptic has its own significance which will be remarked later.

Hitherto, the suppliants have been Jews (if one leaves aside the Samaritan leper). Pointedly, we are now brought to face the prayer of those outside the circle of Israel: a Canaanite woman and a Roman centurion.

> And from there he arose and went away to the region of Tyre and Sidon. And he entered a house, and would not have any one know it; yet he could not be hid. But immediately a woman, whose little daughter was possessed by an unclean spirit, heard of him, and came and fell down at his feet. Now the woman was a Greek, a Syro-Phoenician by birth. And she begged him to cast the demon out of her daughter. And he said to her, "Let the children first be fed, for it is not right to take the children's bread and throw it to the dogs." But she answered him, "Yes, Lord: yet even the dogs under the table eat the children's crumbs." And he said to her, "For this saying you may go your way; the demon has left your daughter." And she went home, and found the child lying in bed, and the demon gone (Mk 7: 24-30; cf Mt 15: 21-28).

This passage is an instance of Mark's special interest in the Gentile mission of the Church—he plays, for all it is worth, any meager indication in the tradition that Jesus did have contact with Gentiles. This woman, "a Greek, a Syro-Phoenician by birth," that is, a Gentile both by birth and by religion, nevertheless comes to Jesus and, like Jairus, pleads for her daughter. A point of the story is that Jesus (v 27) respected the right (acknowledged too by Paul) of the Jews to hear the good news before any others. The woman took up Jesus' word and grounded her plea upon it (v 28). Jesus bows to the woman's faith and assures her that her child is already healed. If Jesus had yielded to this cry of faith even while the division between Jew and Gentile still stood, how much more, Mark seems to be saying, must the Christian church go out to the Gentiles now that Jesus had laid down his life as a ransom "for many" (10: 45), had poured out his blood "for many" (14: 24). Jesus had broken down the barrier between the two peoples (Eph 2: 14).

We have heard two fathers and a mother plead for their children; now a soldier pleads for his servant (his slave as Luke has it): "Lord, my servant is lying paralyzed at home, in terrible distress" (Mt 8: 6; cf Lk 7: 2). When Jesus offered to come and heal the patient, this centurion replied, with words that have remained so familiar to Christians: "Lord, I am not worthy to have you come under my roof; but only say the word, and my servant will be healed" (8: 8). Then Jesus paid the lovely compliment: "Truly I say to you, not even in Israel have I found such faith" (8: 10). It is a faith like that of Mary: "Be it done unto me." There is no suggestion of putting the Lord to the test.

Prayer to Jesus

It cannot fail to be of special interest to us when the disciples pray to Jesus. They turn to him when they are in distress.

> And when he got into the boat, his disciples followed him. And behold, there arose a great storm on the sea, so that the boat was being swamped by the waves; but he was

asleep. And they went and woke him, saying, "Save us, Lord; we are perishing." And he said to them, "Why are you afraid, O men of little faith?" Then he rose and rebuked the winds and the sea; and there was a great calm. And the men marveled, saying, "What sort of man is this, that even winds and sea obey him?" (Mt 8: 23-27; cf Mk 4: 35-41; Lk 8: 22-25).

The scene is vivid—though not, by a long way, as striking as that of Mark (Mk 4: 35-41). The call of the disciples, in the midst of the great storm, is to the one who alone can save them: "Save us, Lord; we are perishing." But it is a call more of desperation than of faith: "Why are you afraid, O men of little faith?" They ought to have rested in the fact that the Lord was with them—that should have been enough.

After all, it is not the little handful of disciples in that lake drama who are chiefly in question. This scene where the disciples are awake and in danger while their Master "sleeps" reflects the post-Easter experience of the Church. Christians may feel that the Lord has no care for them, has abandoned them, and the Church may seem to be at the mercy of the forces pitted against it. Individuals or communities who feel so earn the rebuke, "Have you no faith?"—in Mark's no-nonsense version (Mk 4: 40). It is enough that he should "awaken," that they should have faith and trust in his presence for the storm of their fear to be stilled.

Closely related is the despairing plea of Peter as he began to sink into the waters of the lake. The story is true to what we know of Peter: his impetuosity and his weakness. Again the disciples are in the boat, struggling against wind and wave. Suddenly, the Master appears, walking on the waters (Mt 14: 22-27; Mk 6: 45-52). At that point Matthew adds an episode involving Peter alone.

And Peter answered him, "Lord, if it is you, bid me come to you on the water." He said, "Come." So Peter got out of the boat and walked on the water and came to Jesus; but when he saw the wind, he was afraid, and beginning to sink he cried out, "Lord, save me." Jesus immediately reached out his hand and caught him, saying to him, "O man of little faith, why did you doubt?" And when they got into the boat, the wind ceased. And those in the boat worshiped him, saying, "Truly you are the Son of God" (Mt 14: 28-33).

"Lord, bid me come to you on the water"—that, as it turns out, is the prayer of presumption. There are times when we feel as confident as Peter, ready for whatever the Lord might ask of us. Perhaps it was an experience like that of Peter which made Paul so sure of the true situation: "When I am weak, then I am strong" (2 Cor 12: 10). Our wisest prayer is always that of a Peter made painfully aware of his frailty: "Lord, save me" (Mt 14: 30). That is a prayer that leaves us open and vulnerable to the mercy of the Lord.

Be Merciful to Me, a Sinner

One would be tempted to hope that Peter had learnt his lesson. If we could place the incident of Luke 5: 3-11 after that of Matthew 14: 28-33, we would get that neat sequence. Today we are well aware that any such harmonization is not warranted. As the gospels stand, the probability is that this very humble Peter of Luke anticipates the overconfident Peter of Matthew. The refreshing truth about us humans is that we are unpredictable. We ought to learn our lessons; we ought to move, if not straightly, at least with some constancy, from A to Z. But, of course, we do not. And that is one reason why history is fascinating. People ought to act in such a manner—but there is no guarantee that they will do so. The Bible proves that He who made us takes our unpredictability for granted. It is we ourselves who try to press ourselves and others into a pattern.

If we have any understanding at all of humankind, we will not be disconcerted by the emergence of a Peter very different from him we have just encountered. Jesus, by the

Lake of Gennesareth, stepped into Simon's boat. When he had preached from that podium he bade Simon push out and cast his nets. The blunt fisherman, who had had a bad night, still, unhesitatingly, put out at Jesus' bidding. The result was astounding (Lk 5: 6-7). At that point the impetuous Peter cried out: "Depart from me, for I am a sinful man O Lord" (Lk 5: 8). This is the most Christian prayer of Peter in the gospels. It is the closest to the prayer of the tax collector in the parable-teaching of Jesus: "O God, be merciful to me a sinner." It is too bad that, so very soon, the Christian church, and, notably, the leaders of that church, began to take for granted that God was on their side.

The Lord

The disciples could be more positive:

> The apostles said to the Lord, "Increase our faith." And the Lord said, "If you have faith as a grain of mustard seed, you could say to this sycamine tree, 'Be rooted up, and be planted in the sea,' and it will obey you" (Lk 17: 5-6).

Already, for Luke, Jesus is "Lord": he consistently introduces this post-resurrection title into his gospel. Here the disciples ("apostles" for Luke) ask for a greater confidence in God. It is the quality of faith that matters: a grain of authentic faith—sheer confidence in God—can achieve great things. In Matthew (17: 20) and Mark (11: 23) reference is to the removal of "this mountain." Luke's version represents the Greek idea that nature cannot change: trees do not grow in the sea. Faith and the faithful prayer can achieve the impossible. For faith is openness to God, and with God all things are possible. Confident prayer is based on a faith which believes that God gives even before man asks.

Jesus, Remember Me

The most poignant prayer of all is not from a disciple of Jesus but from an involuntary companion of his suffering: Luke's "good thief."

> One of the criminals who were hanged railed at him, saying, "Are you not the Christ? Save yourself and us!" But the other rebuked him saying, "Do you not fear God, since you are under the same sentence of condemnation? And we indeed justly; for we are receiving the due reward of our deeds; but this man has done nothing wrong." And he said, "Jesus, remember me when you come in your kingly power." And he said to them, "Truly I say to you, today you will be with me in Paradise" (Lk 23: 39-43).

In place of Mark's (15: 32-33) brief statement that both men crucified with Jesus joined in reviling him, Luke declares that only one acted so. The other acknowledges the innocence of Jesus. It would seem that, in Luke's eyes, these two men symbolize Jews and Romans in their attitude to Jesus. The former, like the Jews, seeks in Jesus a Messiah who would arrive in power and dramatically deliver Israel—and rejects him when these hopes are dashed (cf Lk 22: 67-71). The other, like Pilate, admits that Jesus has done nothing wrong, and does not deny his Kingship (cf 23: 3-4). Further, he recognizes Jesus as Messiah. He asks to be remembered when Jesus comes in his kingly power (or into his kingdom), that is, when he comes to inaugurate the messianic age, an event which, in Jewish belief, would involve the resurrection of the dead.

Jesus, the Saviour, assures the "good thief" that his prayer will be answered more promptly than he could have dreamed: this very day, after death, he will enter with Jesus into the life of God; he will be with Christ in the abode of happiness conjured up by the word Paradise—the heavenly dwelling-place (cf 16: 22-26). Clearly "paradise" is an image. Instead of trying to situate "Paradise"—or to imagine it—it is more profitable to recall the words of Ambrose: *Vita est enim esse cum Christo; ideo ubi Christus, ibi vita, ibi regnum.* [Life means being with Christ. Where Christ is, there is life and there is the kingdom.] If Ambrose sounds profound it is only because he is echoing Paul: "My desire is to depart and be with Christ, for that is far better" (Phil 1: 23). "Jesus, remember me . . ." It is a prayer of every Christian. And, in a setting of properly focused Mariology, it is our familiar prayer of everyday: "Holy Mary, Mother of God, pray for us sinners, now, and at the hour of our death." She calls on her Son to remember us and take us into Paradise.

Only by Prayer

The disciples, during Jesus' absence on the mount of Transfiguration, had signally failed to heal a sick boy who had been brought to them for healing. Now, in desperation, the father turns to the Master:

> "If you can do anything, have pity on us and help us." And Jesus said to him, "If you can! All things are possible to him who believes." Immediately the father of the child cried out and said, "I believe; help my unbelief!" (Mk 9: 22-24)

"But if you can do anything"—the man had been discouraged by the failure of the disciples. We must ask ourselves to what extent, still, the failure of disciples leads those who need and seek help to lose confidence in the Master. "If you can!"—Jesus fixes upon the lack of faith. "All things are possible to him who believes": not that faith can do anything, but that faith will set no limits to the power of God. "I believe; help my unbelief": the man acknowledges that his faith is defective. For its strengthening and growth it needs the help of the Master—the Christian overtones are obvious.

The boy was healed (9: 25-27). Then "in the house"—a Marcan device for underlining a message pointedly directed at the Christian—the disciples sought to know why they had failed.

> And when he had entered the house, his disciples asked him privately, "Why could we not cast it out?" And he said to them, "This kind cannot be driven out by anything but prayer" (9: 28-29).

The boy was an epileptic. But according to the understanding of the time his illness was caused by an evil spirit which had to be "cast out." In this context, Jesus explains why the disciples had been unable to cope with the unclean spirit: prayer is vitally necessary, for the exorcist must rely on the power of God. The theme of the powerlessness of the disciples is a further pastoral instruction to the church. The evangelist makes clear that, without Jesus, the disciples are helpless. Christians must seek to find union with him in prayer if they are to share in his power and have part in his work.

Blessing

Even during his ministry, Jesus was an occasion of blessing. Luke, with his delicate feeling for womanhood, has the charming compliment of a mother to the mother of an illustrious son:

> Blessed is the womb that bore you, and the breasts that you sucked (Lk 11: 27).

The idea is thoroughly Jewish: a woman's joy in her son, especially a distinguished son (Gen 30: 13; Prov 23: 25). It is, of course, true that Jesus seemed to turn that compliment: "Blessed rather are those who hear the word of God and keep it!" (Lk 11: 28). But, for Luke the mother of the Lord is supremely a hearer and doer of the Word. We, as his disciples, should strive to be like her.

One might remark that it is natural for a woman to advert to the inescapable fact that the most masculine he-man has to be born of a mother. Yet, one feels that this woman's cry is given depth by the observation of a man—Paul: "In the Lord woman is not independent of man nor man of woman; for as woman was made from man, so man is now born of woman" (1 Cor 11: 11-12). There should be no second-class citizens in the church of Christ. Obviously, we have a long way to go.

Jesus himself was blessed on his entry into the holy city:

> And the crowds that went before him and that followed him shouted, "Hosanna to the Son of David! Blessed be he who comes in the name of the Lord! Hosanna in the highest!" (Mt 21: 9).

Mark's account of this messianic entry is so different (Mk 11: 1-11), quite low-key. Yet, even he shows it to be a moment of significance when the Messiah-King came to his city. For Matthew it is, without apology, the acclamation of the Messiah. We are not too far removed from the incarnate divine one of John. This Matthaean scene is repeated today in our *Corpus Christi* processions, as we acclaim the one who has come.

THE FOURTH GOSPEL

The second part of the Fourth Gospel (chs 13-20) is aptly called the Book of Glory. The theme of it is that, to those who accept him, Jesus shows his glory by his return to the Father in the "hour" of crucifixion—resurrection—ascension. Figuring prominently is the Last Discourse of Jesus (13: 31-16: 33). Here Jesus speaks of his departure and of the future of his disciples, and then of the life of the disciples, and their encounter with the world after his departure. In keeping with our interest, we look to what Jesus has to say about prayer in his name. We should be aware that, more than ever now (for this is the gospel of John with its "high" Christology) we are dealing with an awareness, grown deeper and more keen, of the place of the Lord Jesus in the life of the Christian.

> Whatever you ask, in my name, I will do it, that the Father
> may be glorified in the Son; if you ask anything in my
> name, I will do it (Jn 14: 13-14).

For John, a Christian is one in union with Jesus, a
branch of the True Vine (15: 1-10). In view of this union,
he will pray in Jesus' name. And because Jesus, in his turn,
is one with the Father ("I and the Father are one," 10: 30),
the Christian's prayer will be granted. The presupposition
is that the Christian is conscious of his union with the Son
and, through him, of union with the Father. That conviction, properly awe-inspiring, will ensure that his prayer is
not banal. He will not be petty and seek what may serve in
the short-term. His prayer will have to do with the work of
God that the Son had come to do, the work that had
glorified the Father (17: 4). The concern of his prayer will
be the fuller living of the Christian way. The Father cannot
but heed the prayer of a child which is in harmony with the
desire and will of the Son who had come for one purpose:
"My food is to do the will of him who sent me, and to ac-
complish his work" (4: 34). "I will do it"—Jesus is the
Beloved Son, who alone knows the Father (1: 18). He can,
and will, grant a prayer that the Father would hear.

> If you abide in me, and my words abide in you, ask
> whatever you will, and it shall be done for you...You did
> not choose me, but I chose you and appointed you that you
> should go and bear fruit and that your fruit should abide;
> so that whatever you ask the Father in my name, he may
> give it to you (15: 7, 16).

Whereas, above in 14: 13-14, prayer is addressed directly
to Jesus, here and in chapter 16 the prayer is to the Father,
in Jesus' name. Because of the union of Father and Son it
comes to the same thing. This difference in approach is
because the Farewell Discourse (chs 13-16) is really two
discourses, or two parallel versions of a discourse: chapters
13-14 and 15-16. The ground of prayer is spelled out: abide
in me (15: 7). The image of the vine (15: 1-6) presented
Jesus as the source of real life, a life that can be shared on-

ly by one who is one with him. The following verses (7-17)
bring out the implications of that union. Because he is one
with the Son, whatever the disciples ask will be granted by
the Father. It is assumed that the disciple, chosen and sent
by Jesus himself, "will bear much fruit, and so prove to be
my disciple" (v 8), will be a disciple in truth. "Ask...and it
shall be done for you" (v 7) now carries its full
weight: those who are one with Jesus are his chosen and
loved ones. How can the Father not listen to their prayer!

> Amen, amen, I say to you, if you ask anything of the
> Father, he will give it to you in my name. Hitherto you
> have asked nothing in my name; ask, and you will receive,
> that your joy may be full. I have said this to you in figures;
> the hour is coming when I shall no longer speak to you in
> figures but tell you plainly of the Father. In that day you
> will ask in my name; and I do not say to you that I shall
> pray the Father for you; for the Father himself loves you,
> because you have loved me and have believed that I came
> from the Father (16: 23-27).

There is a clear-cut distinction: "hitherto...in that
day," a distinction brought about through the coming of
"the hour"—the decisive hour of death-and-resurrection.
"In that day" is the time after the resurrection, the time of
the church. Manifestly, *we* are the disciples of "that day."
Our union with Jesus—the Vine—assures us of the loving
attention of our Father. The presupposition is always that
prayer will bear on what makes for a richer Christian life.
This is borne out in 14: 16: "I will pray the Father, and he
will give you another Paraclete, to be with you for ever."
The Paraclete, the Holy Spirit, is the new, abiding presence
of their Lord. This is the supreme gift to them for which
Jesus himself prays on their behalf. Note the interesting
parallel in Luke 11: 13—"how much more will the heavenly Father give the Holy Spirit to those who ask him!"
Prayer for the Holy Spirit sets the tone for all our Christian
asking.

Jesus, who has passed out of this life to the Father, has
not left us orphans; he is with us as Paraclete, as our whol-

ly sympathetic Advocate (1 Jn 2: 1; Heb 7: 25). One with the risen Jesus, the Christian has union with the Father; he will ask in Jesus' name (Jn 16: 23) and the Father will grant in Jesus' name (v 24). This confident asking is "in that day" because it is only after the hour of passion-death-resurrection and giving of the Spirit that the disciple can be fully united with Jesus. The Christian will ask confidently, but in seemly manner, as a child of God. He will ask only for what befits his status. And the answer will bring him joy (v 24) as it leads him into a deeper understanding of Jesus and of the loving Father he has revealed.

This surely is a profound exposition of prayer.

My Lord and My God

The episode of Thomas (20: 24-29) is of great importance for the fourth evangelist and is, indeed, climactic in his gospel.(Chapter 20 is the close of the gospel proper, chapter 21 being an appendix.) The disciple, Thomas, passes from unbelief to belief. The last word of a disciple in the gospel is a full-blooded christological profession of faith.

Thomas refuses to accept the word of the other disciples and insists on having concrete proof of the reality of the resurrection of Jesus (20: 24-25). In the event, Thomas comes to belief without a need for the crude verification he seemed to demand (20: 25, 27-28). It was enough to have *seen* (v 29a; cf vv 20, 25). It is unfortunate that Thomas has been remembered for his stubbornness—"doubting Thomas." He ought to have been remembered for the most forthright confession of faith in the gospels: "My Lord and my God." It is the supreme christological conviction: Jesus may, by Christians, be addressed in the same terms that Israel had addressed Yahweh. The risen Lord is worthy of worship.

Thomas has made the last utterance of a disciple of Jesus. The evangelist adds a comment that is crucial for all disciples of the risen Lord—those of us who live in "that day."

Have you believed because you have seen me? Blessed are
those who have not seen and yet believe (20: 29).

The evangelist is writing for a generation that has not
"seen" the Lord. He would insist that Thomas and the
later disciple are equal, sharing the same blessedness
through their common faith in the Lord. It is this faith that
matters—faith in the sure presence of the Lord, though it
be not visible. It is the tranquil assurance of union with
him.

Come to Me

Perhaps we might end this chapter on a quieter note.
True, the confession of Thomas is a magnificent statement
of faith. And the assurance that the confession can be ours
is our comfort. There is a comforting glow in the gentle invitation of Matthew's Jesus:

> Come to me, all who labor and are heavy laden, and I will
> give you rest. Take my yoke upon you, and learn from me;
> for I am gentle and lowly in heart, and you will find rest
> for your souls. For my yoke is easy, and my burden is light
> (Mt 11: 28-30).

A two-fold invitation is matched by a two-fold promise.
Or, rather, the invitation is "come...and take," and the
promise is "rest." Jewish rabbis spoke of the "yoke of the
Torah"—a yoke which, because of the unwieldy "tradition
of men" raised on the law of Moses (cf Mk 7: 6-18), had
become an intolerable burden (Acts 15: 10). The "yoke"
of Jesus is the demand for love of God and neighbor (Mt
22: 34-40)—"and his commandments are not
burdensome" (1 Jn 5: 3). His yoke is easy and his burden is
light because of who he is—one "gentle and lowly in
heart." He is no taskmaster but a Master who is a Friend
(Jn 15: 14-15). In *his following* is rest to be sought and
found. He had found his "meat," his fulfillment, in doing
the will of the Father (Jn 4: 34). In that will is the disciple
of the Son to find his rest.

Eleven

Prayer of Paul

It should not surprise us that Paul has quite a lot to teach us about prayer. Of all disciples of the Lord he, as far as we know, has been the most faithful. What Paul has to teach in this, as in any area of his concern, must be taken with the utmost seriousness.

In Paul we have to do with a committed Jew, with one who, before he had ever heard of the Christian way, was a man of prayer. The difference that made all the difference was that he progressed from being an observer of the law to one who exulted in the freedom of the way of Jesus. This transformation of Saul the Pharisee into Paul the Christian goes far beyond the realm of prayer. One is saddened by the evidence that the church of our day seems bent on turning the Christian into a bland one-dimensional man. The hope of the optimist—and the optimist has Paul on his side—is broad enough to harbor both the timid ecclesiastic and the hardy prophet. It may be that prayer, as Paul understands it, would transform the one and strengthen the other.

Paul, we know, was a believing Jew, a convinced Pharisee (Phil 3: 5-6). It goes without saying that he prayed. Now become a Christian, he continued to be a man of prayer. The difference is that, henceforth, his prayer is colored by his Christian faith.

Thanksgiving

Paul's "epistles" are letters. He opens in the conventional letter-form of his time: "Paul, to N., greeting"; but conventional in framework only, for he regularly fills out that initial address. Then comes a distinctive feature: thanksgiving. Only in the letter to Galatia does he fail to render thanks, and that is because he is so mad at the Galatians that he wades into them without ceremony: "I am astonished..."(1: 6). Elsewhere he always, at the start, thanks God, fervently and, it may be, at length. In that, his Jewish heritage shows, for Jewish prayer is characterized by thanksgiving—praise of God.

There is no need to look at all of the thanksgiving formulas; a selection will serve quite well. It makes sense to begin with Paul's earliest letter—1 Thessalonians.

> We give thanks to God always for you all, constantly mentioning you in our prayers, remembering before our God and Father your work of faith and labor of love and steadfastness of hope in our Lord Jesus Christ (1 Thess 1: 2-3).

The Apostle gives glory to God for his manifest goodness to this community. He gives thanks for the Christian works of the community inspired by their faith, hope and charity and by a firm confidence in their Lord Jesus Christ. He also makes petition to God on their behalf.

> I give thanks to God always for you because of the grace of God which was given you in Christ Jesus, that in every way you were enriched in him with all speech and all knowledge—even as the testimony to Christ was confirmed among you—so that you are not lacking in any spiritual gift, as you wait for the revealing of our Lord Jesus Christ...God is faithful, by whom you are called into the fellowship of his Son, Jesus Christ our Lord (1 Cor 1: 4-9).

Again, this is primarily a thanksgiving for the gifts conferred by God on the Corinthian community, gifts that

have come to them through Christ—for they belong to him
(3: 23; 6: 15), they are his body (11: 17). He thanks God
that they have been endowed with the charismatic gifts (vv
5, 7), which confirm the truth of the good news of Christ
(v 7). They await the parousia, the revelation of Christ in
glory and power; Paul prays that they will be blameless
before him at his coming (cf Mk 13: 27, 33). He prays
because their blamelessness must be God's achievement,
not their own doing (v 9).

> I thank my God in all my remembrance of you, always in
> every prayer of mine for you all making my prayer with
> joy, thankful for your partnership in the gospel from the
> first day until now. And I am sure that he who began a
> good work in you will bring it to completion at the day of
> Jesus Christ. It is right for me to feel thus about you all,
> because I hold you in my heart, for you are all partakers
> with me of grace, both in my imprisonment and in the
> defense and confirmation of the gospel. For God is my
> witness, how I yearn for you all with the affection of
> Christ Jesus (Phil 1: 3-8).

Here thanksgiving is shot through with joy, for the
Philippians were especially dear to Paul. They had been his
staunchest friends and supporters and he had a tender rap-
port with them, concretely expressed in the fact that, in
their regard, he relaxed his otherwise inflexible rule, and
permitted them to contribute to his support (4: 15-18). His
fervent thanksgiving for the grace manifest in Philippi is
sparked by his affection for this community (v 8). His conviction is that the God who has begun such an auspicious
work will surely have brought it to full flowering when the
Lord comes, in power and glory, to welcome his elect.

The theme of thanksgiving is not confined to the in-
troductory section of the letters but crops up in other
places as well. In 1 Thessalonians 2: 13 Paul thanks God
that the Thessalonians received the word of the good news
which he preached not as a human teaching but as word of
God. He is sure that his response will not match the joy
they have brought him (3: 9). Paul writes of resurrection in

1 Corinthians 15. It might seem that the enslaving powers of Law and Sin and Death must have the last word. But it is not so: "The sting of death is sin, and the power of sin is the law—but thanks be to God, who gives us the victory through our Lord Jesus Christ" (1 Cor 15: 56-57). The sting of death has been drawn by Christ. Death is unable to wound us fatally any more. This is the paradox of resurrection. In his second letter to the Corinthians, the apostle thanks God who has numbered his apostolic preachers in the victory parade of Christ—through them manifesting to the world the triumph of Christ (2 Cor 2: 14).

Petition

Thanksgiving and the prayer of petition are closely linked in the charmingly personal note to Philemon. Paul's prayer contains a generous compliment to Philemon but is also shrewdly calculated to make his plea for the slave Onesimus one that can not, in decency, be ignored.

> I thank my God always when I remember you in my prayers, because I hear of your love and of the faith which you have toward the Lord Jesus and all the saints, and I pray that the sharing of your faith may promote the knowledge of all the good that is ours in Christ (Philemon 4-6).

Paul informs the Thessalonians that he prays earnestly night and day that he might be enabled to come to them and strengthen their faith (1 Thess 3: 10). He gives the text of his prayer:

> Now may our God and Father himself, and our Lord Jesus, direct our way to you; and may the Lord make you increase and abound in love to one another and to all men, as we do to you, so that he may establish your hearts unblamable in holiness before our God and Father, at the coming of our Lord Jesus with all his saints (1 Thess 3: 11-13).

It is a threefold prayer: that Paul may return to Thessalonica; that love, in the community, may grow deeper and spread out more widely; that these Christians may be ready to welcome the Lord when he comes. We must have noted the recurring theme of expectation of the coming of the Lord, an expectation current in the early Church. It is the sole wish of a little prayer interestingly preserved for us in Aramaic: *Maranatha* (1 Cor 16: 22), that is, "Our Lord, come!" This will re-emerge as the last prayer in our New Testament: "Come, Lord Jesus!" (Rev 22: 20).

In the second letter to the Thessalonians Paul again prays for the community:

> We always pray for you, that our God may make you worthy of his call, and may fulfill every good resolve and work of faith by his power, so that the name of our Lord Jesus may be glorified in you, and you in him, according to the grace of our God and the Lord Jesus Christ (2 Thess 1: 11-12).

The Thessalonians had been called from paganism to know and serve the only God. They are fully resolved to live the faith and bear its fruits. Paul prays that God may help them in their resolve and further their works, in order that they may be worthy and eloquent witnesses of the Lord Jesus.

> May the Lord direct your hearts to the love of God and to the steadfastness of Christ (3: 5).

"Steadfastness" (*hypomene*) is faithful endurance: the virtue of those who suffer patiently and firmly for the truth. The prayer is that the Christians may be led further along the road of love of God and patient endurance after the model of Christ.

Paul's affection for his Philippians is the motivation of his warm prayer for them:

> It is my prayer that your love may abound more and more, with knowledge and all discernment, so that you may approve what is excellent, and may be pure and blameless for the day of Christ, filled with the fruits of righteousness which come through Jesus Christ, to the glory and praise of God (Phil 1: 9-11).

The burden of this prayer is that these Christians be filled with the blessings that should flow from their union with Jesus Christ. They will grow into a more perceptive knowledge of the Christian way, looking always for the most Christian course of action. Then they will be happily ready to meet the Lord when he comes.

Paul mentions, more than once, his concern to pray for the communities. In Romans he makes the assertion with emphasis:

> For God is my witness, whom I serve with my spirit in the gospel of his Son, that without ceasing, I mention you always in my prayers, asking that somehow by God's will I may now at last succeed in coming to you (Rom 1: 9-10).

There is something oddly touching in that the solemn assurance that he prays continually for the Roman Christians is followed by his admission that he had prayed, too, that he might be led to visit them. And yet he is not inconsistent; he knows that by his coming to them he can help them (v 11).

The Apostle himself asks for prayer. This is most simply expressed at the close of 1 Thessalonians: "Brethren, pray for us" (5: 25). In the second letter he states the purpose of the community's prayer on his behalf:

> Finally, brethren, pray for us, that the word of the Lord may speed on and triumph, as it did among you, and that we may be delivered from wicked and evil men (2 Thess 3: 1-2).

The prayer is for the progress of Paul's missionary work: that he may be sheltered and that God will bring about the growth of the plant that Paul has sown (cf 1 Cor 3: 5-7). Or again:

> I appeal to you, brethren, by our Lord Jesus Christ and by the love of the Spirit, to strive together with me in your prayers to God on my behalf, that I may be delivered from the unbelievers in Judea, and that my service to Jerusalem may be acceptable to the saints, so that by God's will I may come to you with joy and be refreshed in your company (Rom 15: 30-32).

Paul had long made his special concern a collection for the support of the mother-community of Jerusalem. A generous contribution by the Gentile churches (Gal 2: 10; 1 Cor 16: 1-4; 2 Cor 8:1-9:15), he was convinced, would do much to foster good relations between these communities and the needy Jerusalem church. So important was the matter in his eyes that he had decided to convey their gift in person (Rom 15: 25). Consequently, he asks the Roman Christians to pray that no harm may befall him at the hands of those who are still opposed to him (cf Acts 9: 29; 21: 11); that the collection may be received in the spirit he proposed; and, again, that he might come to Rome in joyous circumstances.

Blessing

The Pauline letters frequently close with a blessing:

> Peace and mercy be upon all who walk by this rule, upon the Israel of God...The grace of our Lord Jesus Christ be with your Spirit, brethren. Amen (Gal 6: 16, 18).

By "the Israel of God" is meant the new Christian people of God standing over against "Israel according to the flesh" (1 Cor 10: 18)—the Jews. The "rule" by which Christians live is the rule of the Spirit (Gal 4: 6-7; 5: 16, 23) and their way is the following of the cross of Christ (2: 20; 5: 24; 6: 14).

> The grace of the Lord Jesus be with you. My love be with you all in Christ Jesus. Amen (1 Cor 16: 23-24).

The interesting point here is the assurance of "my love" for the Corinthian community. So much of the letter had been taken up with the demands of love, and the primacy of love had been so eloquently stressed (ch 13), that Paul cannot leave his readers without a protestation of his love for them in Christ Jesus.

> The grace of the Lord Jesus Christ and the love of God and the fellowship of the Holy Spirit be with you all (2 Cor 13: 14).

To our ears the blessing sounds unmistakably trinitarian; it is not clear that Paul would have regarded it so. But this does remain the richest blessing in his letters: it includes all that is necessary for the salvation of the Christian—divine grace and love and fellowship.

Doxology

Our familiar "Glory be..." has a venerable background. It might seem pretentious to qualify it with the label "doxology"—but that is what it is, a word of glory, a giving glory to God. Paul, as a Jew, is well read in all forms of prayer, no less in doxology than any.

One feels that he has happily hit on a fitting conclusion to a letter instinct with joy, that to the Philippians:

> To our God and Father be glory for ever and ever, Amen (Phil 4: 20).

And there is his ending to the letter to the Romans:

> Now to him who is able to strengthen you according to my gospel and the preaching of Jesus Christ, according to the revelation of the mystery which was kept secret for long ages but is now disclosed and through the prophetic writings is made known to all nations, according to the command of the eternal God, to bring about obedience to

the faith—to the only wise God be glory for evermore through Jesus Christ! Amen (Rom 16: 25-27).

Paul blesses the only wise God, but he does so through Jesus Christ. This God, he is sure, in accordance with the good news Paul has preached—that is to say, Jesus Christ—and in keeping with the "mystery," the divine plan of salvation which embraces all, Jew and Gentile alike, will grant his readers constancy in their living the Christian way. God will bring about "obedience of faith," personal commitment to him who is the subject of Paul's preaching—Jesus Christ.

Scattered throughout the Pauline letters are hymns such as the praise of charity (1 Cor 13), the little hymn to God's mercy (Rom 11: 33-36), and the great Philippian hymn (Phil 2: 6-11), an earlier hymn taken over by Paul. These we leave aside—for somewhat the same reason that we set aside the bulk of the Old Testament psalms.

After Paul

It goes without saying that those epistles which purport to be Pauline will have basically the same structure as the Pauline letters we have seen. We may leave aside, then, such features as thanksgiving and blessing which echo the same features in Paul. We shall look only to what is new or memorable.

In Colossians 4: 2-4 an admonition to perseverance in prayer flows into a plea that the Christian preacher ("Paul," a prisoner) may be freed to proclaim Christ and his saving work for all, for Jew and Gentile, and flows again into a prayer that the preaching may have the persuasive force of clarity.

> Continue steadfastly in prayer, being watchful in it with thanksgiving, and pray for us also, that God may open to us a door for the word, to declare the mystery of Christ, on account of which I am in prison, that I may make it clear, as I ought to speak (Col 4: 2-4).

The author of Ephesians prays that his readers may understand the "mystery"—God's salvation offered to all, without distinction, through Christ. It is a reality grasped only by and through faith, hence the need of prayer for an understanding of the mystery.

> I do not cease to give thanks for you, remembering you in my prayers, that the God of our Lord Jesus Christ, the Father of glory, may give you a spirit of wisdom and of revelation in the knowledge of him, having the eyes of your hearts enlightened, that you may know the hope to which he has called you (Eph 1: 16-18).

It is worthwhile to give a solemn prayer of "Paul," complete with closing doxology. "Paul" kneels, instead of adopting the more usual posture of standing—his prayer is intense. He prays that the Father, through the power of the Spirit, may bring Christ to dwell in these, his disciples, through their faith in him. He prays that through their own experience of a Christian life lived in love they may come at last to appreciate the wonder of the love of Christ for them. For only so can they arrive at an understanding of a God who is love. The doxology (vv 20-21) acknowledges the extraordinary generosity of God who will always surpass our expectations. An interesting feature here is the setting of Christ and church side by side. It presumes that "church" is truly church of Christ. The Christian churches, it seems, have always much too readily assumed that they are indeed such.

> For this reason I bow my knees before the Father, from whom every family in heaven and on earth is named, that according to the riches of his glory he may grant you to be strengthened with might through his Spirit in the inner man, and that Christ may dwell in your heart through faith; that you, being rooted and grounded in love, may have power to comprehend with all the saints what is the breadth and length and height and depth, and to know the love of Christ which surpasses knowledge, that you may be filled with all the fullness of God. Now to him who by the

power at work within us is able to do far more abundantly than all we ask or think, to him be glory in the church and in Christ Jesus to all generations, for ever and ever. Amen (Eph 3: 14-21).

"Paul" exhorts his readers to pray, whenever they do pray, in the Spirit. That means enlightened prayer, open-eyed and persevering. And he asks for prayer for himself, that he may be a courageous minister of the word. It is noteworthy that Paul and his disciples are so anxious that the Christian communities should pray for their missionaries. The apparently bizarre, but really inspired, selection of a cloistered Carmelite nun [Therese of Lisieux] as patroness of the missions is wholly in line with this New Testament attitude to the Christian mission.

Pray at all times in the Spirit, with all prayer and supplication. To that end keep alert with all perseverance, making supplication for all the saints, and also for me, that utterance may be given me in opening my mouth boldly to proclaim the mystery of the gospel, for which I am an ambassador in chains: that I may declare it boldly, as I ought to speak (Eph 6: 18-20).

The Pastoral Letters

In the pastoral letters (1, 2 Tim, Titus) we need note only 1 Timothy 5: 5. An interesting development in the post-apostolic church was an institution of "widows." The requirements are spelled out: "Let no one be enrolled as a widow who is under sixty years of age, or has been married more than once; and she must be well attested for her good deeds. . ." (1 Tim 5: 9-10). (In parenthesis, one should not fail to see what a prescription for a wide and fruitful Christian ministry one has here: a pastor and minister of the eucharist of mature years, an experienced family person, one whose goodness was known. But we are beset with "prudence"—and the people of God go without the bread of life.) It is expected that these widows are to pray for the rest of us:

> She who is a real widow, and is left alone, has set her hope
> on God and continues in supplications and prayers night
> and day (1 Tim 5: 5).

We might do worse than end this look at the prayer of
Paul and his disciples on this note of widows and their
prayer. A snag is that the image of elderly widow, like that
of cloistered nun, must suggest a subordinate and passive
role of women in the church. I have long felt that only
women themselves can achieve their proper status. And I
have hoped, and do not despair, that woman-power,
powerfully exercised within the Christian community, may
sweep aside the prejudice of centuries. Only when women
find their true, their equal place, can the church truly be
the church of Christ. The luminous and prophetic word of
Paul stands, and will not be gainsaid:

> There is neither male nor female, for you are all one in
> Christ Jesus (Gal 3: 28).

The Spirit of Prayer

Luke has told us that "the heavenly Father will give the
Holy Spirit to those who ask him" (Lk 11: 13). We learn,
from Paul, that the Spirit is our mentor in prayer. More,
the Spirit is the ground of our prayer.

Paul would have Christians face up to the astounding
truth that they, adopted out of love, are God's own
children.

> When the time had fully come, God sent forth his Son,
> born of woman, born under the law, to redeem those who
> were under the law, so that we might receive adoption as
> sons. And because you are sons, God has sent the spirit of
> his Son into our hearts, crying, "Abba! Father!" (Gal
> 4: 4-6).

The apostle evidently feels that we need to be assured of
our status, so unbelievable it must seem. God, through his
Spirit, in his almighty power, has brought us, creatures of

flesh and blood, into his own family. And he has sent "the spirit of his Son" to convince us. Fittingly, he is the Spirit of the Son, of him who was made flesh and pitched his tent among us (Jn 1: 14), who became one of us, like us in all things (Heb 4: 15). This Spirit, speaking to the heart of Christians, assures him and her that they are indeed children of God. The Spirit prays in the Christian, emboldening him or her to address God as "Father," in the same intimate way that Jesus did.

The wonder of divine sonship so affects Paul that when he came to write Romans he repeated that exhortation of Galatians.

> For all who are led by the Spirit of God are children of God. For you did not receive the spirit of slavery to fall back into fear, but you have received the spirit of sonship. When we cry Abba! Father! it is the Spirit himself bearing witness with our spirit that we are children of God (Rom 8: 14-16).

Again, the fact of sonship has its inbuilt logic. The Spirit who brings men into a union of brotherhood with Christ and establishes them in a special relationship of sonship with the Father must, too, bring them to an awareness of this extraordinary situation, one beyond the bounds of human expectation. It is an exercise in Divine courtesy. The God who has adopted us as his children awakens in us an awareness of that fact, and then gently helps us in our wondering acknowledgment of the fact: Abba! It has about it something of the flavour of a mother teaching her little child to pray. There is the same quality of love that strips the exercise of any condescension.

Paul returns to the same theme later on:

> Likewise the Spirit helps us in our weakness; for we do not know how we ought to pray, but the Spirit himself intercedes for us with sighs too deep for words. And he who searches the hearts of men knows what is the mind of the Spirit because the Spirit intercedes for the saints according to the will of God (8: 26-27).

Man is irrevocably human and his aspirations often fight a losing battle with his natural weakness. The Spirit comes to his help, adding to man's prayer his own intercession which transcends human frailty. Without this divine help man could never have the discernment, or the temerity, to address God as his "Abba." It is the will of God, loving Father, that the Christian should not only recognize, but thankfully acknowledge his unbelievable status. The Father knows that only he can bring this about; and so his Spirit speaks to the spirit of man, stirring him to awareness and to joyous confession. God is attuned to the assisted Christian prayer. Once again, the analogy of mother and child. Who can doubt that the lisped prayer of an infant, inspired by a loving parent, is pleasing to God? It is no less prayer because it has been prompted.

Would that we would hearken to the Spirit and dare to do what Son and Father ask. *Audemus dicere*—let us dare! We *are* children of God. Let us then chatter away, incoherently and inconsequentially, to our Abba, for that is the way of children. But let us also listen, when he speaks—for our Dad knows *everything*. That, too, is the way of children.

Twelve

Prayer of the Faithful

The title of this closing chapter is, frankly, phrased broadly enough to contain the New Testament writings which we have not considered up to now. It surely does not suggest that Paul and the others might not be numbered among the faithful.

We look, first, to the Catholic Epistles (James; 1, 2 Peter; 1, 2, 3 John; and Jude), so named because of their "general" character—addressed to Christians in general (and not to individual churches like the letters of Paul). On the whole, these represent the latest stratum of the New Testament. If they have not much to say about prayer that is not because these later Christians did not pray. These letters address situations which call for correction and guidance. One might argue that prayer was not a problem.

The *anawim* (the "poor") emerge in later Judaism: those (many, no doubt, economically poor) who put their whole trust in God. Their attitude is that extolled by Jesus, that of "little children," open and trustful. We have the prayers of Mary, and Simeon, and of the supreme "poor man"—Jesus himself.

The Revelation of John is spangled with heavenly liturgies. As the seer gazes into the heavenly place, he sees the denizens of heaven in worship and hears their songs. His hymns are, or reflect, hymns of the early Church. A departure from our attention to personal rather than liturgical prayer is justified in this closing section. The end of all our prayer is union with the Lord. Prayer gives voice to our yearning to be with him forever—in the heavenly Jerusalem (Rev 21: 22-26).

I. The Faithful

JAMES

The letter of James was written for a milieu in which social inequality was marked. The author's sympathy goes to the weak and afflicted. While he does take issue with injustice, poverty has for him a religious value which makes of the unfortunate the privileged friends of God.

The statement in 4: 8—"Draw near to God and he will draw near to you"—is, at least implicitly, an invitation to prayer. For prayer is a meeting of Father and child.

The passage 5: 13-18 holds an interest beyond that of prayer. But it does firmly underline the place of prayer in the lives of Christians.

> Is anyone among you suffering? Let him pray. Is any cheerful? Let him sing praise. Is any among you sick? Let him call for the elders of the Church, and let them pray over him, anointing him with oil in the name of the Lord; and the prayer of faith will save the sick man, and the Lord will raise him up; and if he has committed sins, he will be forgiven. Therefore confess your sins to one another, and pray for one another, that you may be healed. The prayer of a righteous man has great power in its effects. Elijah was a man of like nature with ourselves and he prayed fervently that it might not rain, and for three years and six months it did not rain on the earth. Then he prayed again, and the earth brought forth its fruit (5: 13-18).

"Suffering" and "cheerful" point to the extremes of human experience. "Pray" and "sing praise" come to the same thing. The Christian is being urged to "pray at all times" (Eph 6: 18). The sick Christian is obviously ill enough to be confined to bed: he must send for the elders. The "elders" are those who hold a position of authority in the church (e.g. Acts 14: 23; 15: 2-6; 1 Tim 5: 17, 19; 1 Peter 5: 1-5). While it would be anachronistic to call them "priests," that same call of the Christian sick of our day is, in practice, answered by a visit of the Christian priest. Already in the Old Testament (Sirach 38: 9-10) prayer to win healing is recommended. These elders pray for the sick man and they anoint him. At the time, anointing the sick as a curative measure was common among Jews and Gentiles (cf Mk 6: 13). The anointing, here, is accompanied by invocation of the Lord Jesus, evoking his healing presence. The prayer is a prayer "of faith," expressive of the conviction that the Lord has the power and the will to save the sick man. "To save" (*sōzein*) does mean restoration to health. Elsewhere in James (1: 21; 2: 14; 4: 12; 5: 20) "to save" means spiritual salvation. In our text, both senses operate: the faithful sick Christian may well be restored to health. He will surely win eternal life. The sequence points to the presence of this further meaning. "The Lord will raise him up" can mean restoration to health, but can also mean something more: a raising up to eternal life. Reference to forgiveness of sins leaves no doubt that James is looking beyond restoration to physical health. That he should do so is in keeping with the Hebrew outlook. Healing must reach to the whole man; restoration to bodily health only could never be enough.

"Sins" acts as a catchword—James goes on to confession of sins. What is in mind is confession of sin as preparation for prayer. We retain this, admittedly in a pale version, in our penitential rite preparatory to the celebration of the Eucharist. Christians are to pray for one another (Mt 5: 44; Acts 12: 5; Col 3: 4; 1 Thes 5: 25; 2 Thes 3: 1; Heb 13: 18). No longer is James addressing the sick. He has turned to Christians in general and "healing" here refers to forgiveness of sins. A new dimension is added. We spontaneously pray for our relatives and friends who are physically ill. We should pray more urgently for those who are spiritually sick—their need is so much the greater. Elijah (1 Kgs 17: 1, 7; 18: 1, 41-45) is presented as a model of efficacious prayer. James is careful to forestall the obvious objection that Elijah was no ordinary person. No, he insists, even Elijah was "a man of like nature with ourselves." The prayer of any Christian, provided it be true prayer, can be as efficacious as the prayer of Elijah.

If prayer for the spiritually ill is especially recommended there is, now, the reward of that prayer. To win back the erring brother is the supreme work of love. The one who achieves this must know that his own sins will be blotted out by a Lord who treasures brotherly love above all else.

1, 2 JOHN

John declares that the purpose of his letter (1 John) is that his disciples may have fellowship with the whole church, a fellowship that flows from their Christian fellowship with the Father and with his Son, Jesus Christ (1 Jn 1: 3). Though he does not say so explicitly, it must follow that a privileged way of fostering fellowship with Father and Son is the way of prayer. John bids his disciples abide in Christ (2: 28). Because the love of God for us is manifest in his Son, there should be no servile fear in our love of God (4: 17-19). We can turn to God, trustingly, as to our Abba.

John closes his letter with a statement of devastating directness:

> This is the testimony, that God gave us eternal life, and this life is in his Son. He who has the Son has life; he who has not the Son has not life (5: 11-12).

Salvation is a free and generous gift of God. That gift has upon it the stamp of divine courtesy: it is offered to us through his beloved Son. Union with the Son, achieved in baptism, is sustained by our prayer.

The second letter of John has a blessing not unlike that of the Pauline letters:

> Grace, mercy and peace will be with us, from God the Father and from Jesus Christ the Father's Son, in truth and love (2 Jn 3).

The presence of the terms truth and love give the blessing a distinctively Johannine cast—"love" and "truth" are key words in these letters.

JUDE

The author of Jude warns that the faithful should not be led astray by erroneous teaching but should cling to the teaching of the apostles. They must not be deceived by "worldly people, devoid of the Spirit" (v 19). Instead, by prayer to the Holy Spirit, they should maintain themselves in the love of God, looking to the mercy of God that leads to eternal life. For the Holy Spirit is present in the believer and prayer must be made in the Holy Spirit (vv 20-21). And Jude provides us with a doxology which suitably rounds off this glance at prayer in the catholic epistles:

> Now to him who is able to keep you from falling and to present you without blemish before the presence of his glory with rejoicing, to the only God, our Saviour, through Jesus Christ our Lord, be glory, majesty, dominion, and authority, before all time and now and for ever. Amen (Jude 24-25).

II. The Poor

The word *anawim* has become familiar to us. At first, in its Hebrew usage, it was a sociological term, designating the economically poor. However, it had taken on a religious tone, referring to the pious man, the committed

Yahwist. The *anawim*, the "Poor Ones," lived out and manifested a distinctive feature of Jewish piety: they were those who did not trust in their own resources but relied in utter confidence upon God. Luke tells us that there were such *anawim* in the early Church. Mary and Simeon are typical representatives of the poor. Jesus himself is the perfect model of the poor. The New Testament canticles, Magnificat and Nunc Dimittis (as well as Benedictus) come from the circles of Jewish-Christian *anawim*. Luke has put these early Christian hymns in the mouths of Mary and Simeon (and Zechariah).

The Magnificat (Lk 1: 46–55)

The narrative of the Visitation (Lk 1: 39-45) serves as a hinge between the two births that figure in Luke's Infancy Gospel (Lk 1-2): of John the Baptist and of Jesus. This meeting between the mothers and their babies illustrates their respective situations, well expressed by the title *Kyrios* (Lord) put by Luke on the lips of Elizabeth: "Why is this granted to me that the mother of my Lord should come to me" (Lk 1: 48).

Mary's reply to the words of Elizabeth (1: 42-45) is the Magnificat:

> My soul glorifies the Lord,
> my spirit rejoices in God my Saviour.
> He looks on his servant in her lowliness;
> henceforth all ages will call me blessed.

> The Almighty works marvels for me.
> Holy his name!
> His mercy is from age to age,
> on those who fear him.

> He puts forth his arm in strength
> and scatters the proud-hearted.
> He casts the mighty from their thrones
> and raises the lowly.

> He fills the starving with good things,
> sends the rich away empty.

He protects Israel, his servant,
remembering his mercy,
the mercy promised to our fathers,
to Abraham and his sons for ever. (Lk 1: 46-55).

This hymn is the conclusion to, and the interpretation of, Luke's Visitation-scene. In form a psalm of thanksgiving, the Magnificat is a chain of Old Testament reminiscences, and leans heavily on the canticle of Hannah (1 Sam 2: 1-10). In it we find no clear reference to the messianic birth—and this is surprising in view of the angel's message (1: 31-35), and the words of Elizabeth. Besides, the "humiliation" (rather than "humility" or "lowliness") does not apply very well to the young virgin. The Magnificat is a psalm that has come to Luke from the circle of the "poor of Yahweh"—*anawim* who may well have been Jewish-Christians. It is not difficult to appreciate that a psalm from the milieu of the *anawim*—whether they be Jews or Jewish followers of Christ—would already marvelously conform to the outlook of this "handmaid of the Lord" (Lk 1: 36). Most likely, the psalm was first found in the mouth of the Daughter of Zion—a personification of the people of God—who, in the prophets, is the spouse of Yahweh, tried, humiliated, helped and delivered, giving birth to the messianic people (Is 54: 1; 66: 7-12; Mi 4: 10; Jer 4: 31) and the Messiah (Is 7: 34; Mi 5: 1-2). The psalm suits Mary who, unmistakably, lives by the spirit of the *anawim*.

First Stanza (1: 46-50)

Elizabeth had blessed Mary as mother of the Messiah; Mary (46-48) gives the glory in joyful thanksgiving to the God who had blessed her and, through her, Israel: "My soul magnifies the Lord." The rest of the opening cry of joy (v 47) echoes the words of Habakkuk: "I will rejoice in the Lord, I will joy in the God of my salvation" (Hb 3: 18; cf 1 Sam 2: 1). God has looked with favour upon his handmaid, upon her who is pre-eminently one of the "poor of

Yahweh." Her total acceptance of God's will (cf 1 Sam
1: 11) has won for her, the favoured one (Lk 1: 28),
everlasting glory. All mankind will find hope in what God
has achieved in Mary: loneliness turned into fruitfulness.
At once (vv 49-50) she turns her attention to the Almighty,
the holy and merciful God (cf Dt 10: 21; Ps 111: 9) who
has done such great things for her. The mighty one shows
his power most of all in caring for the needy. In truth "the
steadfast love of the Lord is from everlasting to everlasting
upon those who fear him" (Ps 103: 17).

Second Stanza (1: 51-53)

The interest now switches to Israel and to the manifestation of God's power, holiness and goodness in favour of
his people. These verses are not concerned with the past, or
not with the past only, but represent God's action at all
times: what he has done to Mary and what he, through her
as mother of the Messiah, has done for Israel, shows forth
his manner of acting. He does mighty deeds with his arm,
the symbol of his power, when he reverses human situations—the proud, the mighty and the rich he has humbled,
destroyed and left empty, while he has raised up and
blessed with good things the poor of this world (the
anawim). None of this, of course, is brought about by a
social revolution which sets one in place of the other; the
change follows on God's attitude toward those who ask
humbly and toward those who believe that they have the
right to demand. The great reversal is finally effected in the
perfect stage of the kingdom, the life to come.

Conclusion (1: 54-55)

These closing verses, in the mouth of Mary, point to the
final intervention of God. His sending of the Messiah is the
crowning act of his gracious testament to Israel, that people which, through his covenant with Abraham (Gen 17: 7)
had become his "servant" (Is 41: 8-9). Mindful of his great

mercy, he has fulfilled the promise made to the patriarch: a promise made to one man is accomplished in one woman.

The Nunc Dimittis (Lk 2: 29-32)

> At last, all-powerful Master,
> you give leave to your servant
> to go in peace, according to your promise.
>
> For my eyes have seen your salvation
> which you have prepared for all nations,
> the light to enlighten the Gentiles
> and give glory to Israel, your people (Lk 2: 29-32).

The canticle of Simeon is a commentary on the presentation of the child Jesus in the temple (2: 22-28), an episode that is obviously of great importance for Luke. For, when we read that passage in the light of 1: 16-17 and Malachi 3: 1, 23, it must follow that the "Holy One" who is presented in the temple is none other than the *Lord*: "Behold, I send my messenger to prepare the way before me, and the Lord whom you seek will suddenly come to his temple" (Mal 3: 1).

Simeon, the righteous and devout, realizes that, in view of the fulfillment of the promise made to him (Lk 2: 26), death must be near; he can die in peace like Abraham (Gen 15: 15), but more privileged than Abraham. His cup of joy has been filled to overflowing because he has gazed upon the "salvation of God," the Messiah whom God has sent to save his people. And not his own people only: the Gentiles are destined for salvation too. This messianic salvation is not only a beacon which shines before the nations, it is a brightness which dissipates their darkness and enlightens them. Salvation is for all.

Jesus

Mary and Simeon are, beyond doubt, worthy representatives of the *anawim*. But the finest exponent of that way

is none other than Jesus himself. We have his attestation:
"I am gentle and lowly in heart" (Mt 11: 29). He can be expected to manifest, in its purest form, the characteristic of
the *anawim*. And he has done so:

> In that same hour he rejoiced in the Holy Spirit and said,
> "I thank thee, Father, Lord of heaven and earth, that thou
> hast hidden these things from the wise and understanding
> and revealed them to babes; yea, Father, for such was thy
> gracious will" (Lk 10: 21; Mt 11: 25-26).

This saying, so reminiscent of John, clearly expresses the
unique relationship of Father and Son. The "wise" are the
leaders of Israel; the "babes" are the simple folk, the
disciples who hear and do—*the anawim*. The secret that
the Father has confided to the humble is the mutual
knowledge of Father and Son, revealed to those whom the
Son chooses. Jesus had said "unless you become as little
children...." A Christian must be open to a Father who
loves—just as simply as a child rushes to the door at a
homecoming and clings to a hand.

III. Prayer in Heaven

The author of the Book of Revelation, a Christian
prophet named John, presents his writing as a "letter" to
be read in the churches (Rev 1: 3). Throughout the book
his interest in liturgy is evident. Most obviously, the many
hymns he gives, though sung by heavenly choirs, reflect the
hymnal tradition of the first-century church.

The seer, transported to heaven (4: 1) hears the four
"living creatures," symbols of the cosmos, sing the canticle
of the seraphim (cf Is 6: 3)—the unceasing song of nature
in praise of the Creator (Rev 4: 8). The twenty-four elders,
representatives of the saints of Israel, join in worship; they
ascribe glory and honour and power to their Lord and
God, the Creator (4: 10-11). In 5: 8-9 the living creatures
and the elders acknowledge the divinity of the Lamb and

offer, as fragrant incense, the prayers of the saints. They sing a new song extolling the redemption wrought by Christ. A countless host of angels joins in praise of the Lamb (5: 11-12). The whole creation raises its voice (5: 13) and the living creatures give their "Amen" (5: 14).

The sound of the seventh trumpet, heralding the end, is answered by loud voices in heaven, the praise of the living creatures and of the angelic choirs (11: 15). The canticle of 11: 17-18, put in the mouths of the twenty-four elders, is thoroughly Jewish in its sentiments and expression; the elders thank God that he has at last manifested his great power—the kingdom of God has come.

A heavenly hymn (12: 10-12) celebrates the downfall of Satan and the triumph of the martyrs, achieved through the blood of the Lamb. The words of the heavenly hymn of 14: 2-3 are not given; only the 144,000 companions of the Lamb know the "new song." The host of martyrs standing beside the heavenly sea sing the song of Moses and of the Lamb—recalling Israel's song of triumph over Egypt on the shore of the Red Sea (15: 3-4; cf Ex 15). The words of an angel (Rev 16: 5-6) form a sort of antiphon to the canticle of 15: 3-4—they vindicate the divine righteousness and holiness proclaimed in the canticle. The martyrs add their "Amen" (16: 7). In 19: 1-3 resounds the mighty sound of the angel host. The acclamation "Hallelujah" ("praise Yahweh") used in synagogue worship, early figured in Christian liturgy. In the New Testament it occurs only in Revelation. To this canticle of the angels, living creatures and elders say their "Amen" (19: 4). The hymn of praise (19: 6-8), sung by the great multitude of martyrs, swells like the roar of waters or like mighty thunder-peals. The faithful rejoice because their earnest prayer—"Thy kingdom come"—has been answered: the Lord reigns. It is a song of exultation because the marriage of the Lamb is at hand. At last, in the new Jerusalem, before the throne of God and the Lamb, the servants of God will worship and will reign as priests forever (22: 3-5). It is worship "in spirit and truth" (Jn 4: 23).

Having outlined the progress of prayer throughout

Revelation, it is well to look at some specific passages. It makes sense to follow the selections from Revelation given in the new Breviary.

Chapter 4 of Revelation ends (4: 6-11) with the first of the heavenly liturgies of the book; it is the setting of the brief canticle, 4: 11—

> Worthy are you our Lord and God,
> to receive glory and honour and power,
> for you created all things,
> and by your will they existed and were created.

All of these canticles are modeled on, or reflect, or simply are, early Christian hymns. Whereas the living creatures had addressed the Creator, rather distantly, as Lord God Almighty (4: 8), the elders see him as *"our* Lord and God." The little hymn of 4: 11, which has nothing specifically Christian about it, is fitting in the mouths of the elders—the saints of Israel.

The sealed scroll which "the one seated on the throne" (5: 1) passed on to the Lamb contains "words of lamentation and mourning and woe" addressed to an Israel that had lost its way. When the Lamb had accepted the scroll (which he alone could unseal), the twenty-four elders who already, in keeping with their cultic role throughout Revelation, had sung the canticle of 4: 11 addressed to the Lord God Almighty, now sing a "new song" in praise of the Lamb:

> Worthy are you, O Lord,
> to take the scroll and to open its seals,
> for you were slain,
> and by your blood you ransomed men for God
> from every tribe and tongue and people and nation.
> You have made us a kingdom and priests to our God,
> and we shall reign on earth (5: 9-10).

The Lamb has "ransomed" men at the cost of his blood. This is a striking metaphor, suggesting both liberation from the slavery of sin and the reality of the demands made on the Saviour. Paul says that Christians have been "bought with a price" (1 Cor 6: 20). A literal understanding of words like "ransom" and "bought" had led to unacceptable theories of redemptive liberation whereby a price (the life of Jesus) was paid to the offended God (or to Satan!). Redemption is an expression of love: "God so *loved* the world that he *gave* his Son" (Jn 3: 16). Salvation is offered to all men and women, "from every tribe and tongue and people and nation." The redeemed are kings and priests as Jesus exercises through them his royal and priestly functions.

The doxology (5: 12), by the countless host of angels (5: 11; cf 7: 10), addressed to the Lamb, is fuller than that which the elders had addressed to the Creator.

> Worthy is the Lamb who was slain,
> to receive power and wealth,
> and wisdom and might,
> and honour and glory and blessing (5: 12).

It is noteworthy that the attributes of the Lamb turn up later in a doxology addressed to God (7: 12).

At the close of the first part of Revelation the twenty-four elders sing another song. They thank and glorify God who has at last manifested his great power: the kingdom of God has come. Up to now, God was "he who is and was and is to come" (1: 4, 8; 4: 8). Here there is no "is to come" (cf 16: 5): he has come, his reign has begun.

> We give thanks to you, Lord God Almighty,
> who are and who were,
> that you have taken your great power
> and begun to reign.
> The nations raged,
> but your wrath came,
> and the time for the dead to be judged,
> for rewarding your servants, the prophets and saints,
> and those who fear your name,
> both small and great (11: 17-18).

The time has come for judging, for rewarding and for destroying. "The kingdom of the world has become the kingdom of our Lord and of his Christ" (11: 15).

The victory of Christ, symbolically shown as a war between Michael and the Dragon (12: 7-9) is followed by rejoicing in heaven:

> Now the salvation and the power
> and the kingdom of our God
> and the authority of his Christ have come,
> for the accuser of our brethren has been thrown down,
> who accuses them day and night before our God.
>
> And they have conquered him
> by the blood of the Lamb
> and by the word of their testimony,
> for they loved not their lives even unto death.
> Rejoice, then, O heaven,
> and you that dwell therein (12: 10-12).

The "brethren" of verse 10 now stand disclosed as the Christian martyrs. They are those "who have come out of the great tribulation" and "have washed their robes...in the blood of the Lamb" (7: 14). They represent all who will shed their blood for Christ all through the time of the Church, which is the time of trial (7: 12, 17). They have conquered Satan "by the blood of the Lamb"—his victory is their victory too (cf 5: 9-10; 7: 9-17). Hence the great rejoicing in heaven.

The opening verse (15: 1) of chapter 5, depicting a scene cast on the screen of heaven, is rather like a heading to the chapter. Standing by the heavenly sea, the conquerors of the beast, the martyrs, sing the "song of Moses" (cf Ex 15: 1).

> Great and wonderful are your deeds,
> O Lord God the Almighty!
> Just and true are your ways,
> O King of the ages!
>
> Who shall not fear and glorify your name, O Lord?
> For you alone are holy.

> All nations shall come and worship you,
> For your judgments have been revealed (15: 3-4).

Unlike the song of the Exodus, the martyrs' song is not one of triumph over their enemies, while it does praise God for their own victory. The deliverance of the Israelites from Egypt was the type of the deliverance of the saints from the Beast. This "song of Moses" is also, and principally, the "song of the Lamb" because the martyrs have won their victory by the blood of the Lamb (7: 14; 12: 11). The canticle itself is a mosaic of Old Testament phrases. The song holds out hope that the nations, in view of the righteous deeds of the Lord, will fear him and render him homage and worship.

In chapter 19 we hear a mighty paean of joy in heaven:

> Hallelujah! The Lord our God, the Almighty reigns.
> Let us rejoice and exult and give him the glory.
> The marriage of the Lamb has come,
> And his bride has made herself ready.
> It was granted her to be clothed with fine linen,
> bright and pure (19: 6-8).

This hymn of praise sounded like the roar of flood waters or like mighty thunder peals. The multitude of martyrs rejoice that their oft-repeated prayer—"Thy kingdom come"—has been answered: The Lord reigns! The saints rejoice because the marriage of the Lamb has come: his bride is ready. Israel as the bride of Yahweh is a prophetic image (Hos 2: 16; Is 54: 6; Ezek 16: 7-8). Paul had transferred the imagery to Christ and his church (2 Cor 11: 2; cf Eph 5: 25, 32). In Ephesians 5: 25 we read that "Christ loved the Church and gave himself up for her"; and, in Revelation, those who form the bride of Christ have been redeemed "by the blood of the Lamb" (5: 9; 7: 14; 14: 3-4).

"It was granted her to be clothed with fine linen, bright and pure" (v 8). In Ephesians 5: 26-27 Christ has prepared his bride by washing her in the bath of baptism and by making her immaculate. Here the situation is quite the

same: "it is granted her to be clothed"—her wedding-dress
is a gift. In Ephesians 5: 26 Christ "sanctified" his bride;
here she "is given" the white bridal dress of holiness.
Always, her sanctity is his achievement. And this remains
so even though John comments: "for the fine linen is the
righteous deeds of the saints" (Rev 19: 8). These righteous
deeds are the sum of the saintly acts of the members of
Christ, wrought in them by the Spirit.

Revelation closes with a prayer: "Come, Lord Jesus!"
(22: 20). This is the Aramaic *maranatha* (1 Cor 16: 22), the
prayer of the Christian as he waits for his Lord. We are
reminded of Paul's earnest wish:

> My desire is to depart and be with Christ,
> for that is far better (Phil 1: 23).

Epilogue

These prayers, of the Old Testament and of the New, are varied, but there is a common factor to them. And that is a profound sense of God's companionship, of his nearness, his taking care of all circumstances. It is a sense of constant communion and fellowship with God as a friend and it becomes most fully realized in Jesus—the Son of God who "pitched his tent" among men.

Companionship

The sense of the companionship of God: it was the secret of Jesus' own prayer life. What moved him to rise a long while before dawn to go out and pray in a lonely place so that he was long absent from his disciples? (cf Mk 1: 35). Or what made him go out "into the hills to pray, and all night he continued in prayer to God"? (Lk 6: 12). In short, what was it that moved him to mark his every prayer with the new, intimate mode of address: *Abba*? It was his abiding sense of communion with the Father, his knowing he was never alone:

> believe me that I am in the Father and the Father in me...the hour is coming when you will all be scattered, every man to his home, and will leave me alone, yet I am not alone, for the Father is with me (Jn 14: 11; 16: 32).

What Jesus felt of his Father's closeness was the intimately personal relationship which the men and women of the Old Testament had felt in various ways toward their God.

That which Jesus felt with his Father was the same companionship his disciples, and all Christians, came to feel in him. This is movingly portrayed in the Emmaus narrative wherein Cleopas and his companion had the comfort of his fellowship when "Jesus himself drew near and went with them"—when he, unknown to them, walked along beside them and then "went in to stay with them" at eventide (Lk 24: 13-35). There, as they broke bread together, they came to recognize their Lord, the one whom they had been given as their Friend. They had opened their door to him, and he came in to sup with them and they with him. He vanished from their sight...but their eyes had been opened—to know he was with them always, and that this itself would be their prayer.

Faith

The basis, the source, of prayer is faith—and the faith is faith in Jesus. It is the believing which is not afraid to ask, because this he wants: "Ask and it shall be given you, seek and you shall find, knock and it shall be opened to you" (Mt 7: 7), for who would give his son a stone if he asked for bread, and will not the heavenly Father even more give to his children the good things of their asking (cf 7: 9-10). After all, he does know what we need before we ask him (cf 6: 8). The little parables of the Friend at Midnight (Lk 11: 5-13) and the Unjust Judge (18: 1-8) teach the importance of asking, of perseverance in prayer.

And because of Jesus, this asking is to be on a new basis. It is the prayer of believing in him, and so it is the prayer of asking in his name:

> Whatever you ask in my name I will do it, that the Father may be glorified in the Son; if you ask anything in my name, I will do it (Jn 14: 13-14).

What is the "anything" we could ask—the anything he will do? It is simply the comfort of his friendship, the joy of his presence, the fullness of life lived with him, and this means leaving our own ways behind. "Hitherto, you asked nothing in my name. Ask, and you will receive, that your joy may be full" (Jn 14: 9). He does not need to pray to the Father for us, Jesus goes on to say, because the Father himself loves us. Because of this love, the Father and Son come to us and make their home with us and within us (cf Jn 14: 23). They do not leave us alone. It is a present answer to the heartfelt, forward-looking prayer of all Christians: *Marana-tha*—Come, Lord Jesus (Rev 23: 30).

We recall again the road to Emmaus: Jesus drew near and went with his disciples. He drew near to the disciples, went with them, and "appeared to be going further"—until they stopped him and asked him, "Stay with us, for it is now toward evening and the day is far spent" (Lk 24: 29). They asked, and so he answered: he went in to stay with them, he became known to them in the breaking of the bread, and he opened their eyes. "Stay with us": this, at heart, is the recurrent prayer of the Bible, the longing of the psalmist who wanted to dwell in the Lord's house all the days of his life. "Stay with us": it is the prayer ever answered by our believing, "Lo, I am with you always...."